T0113399

YOUR PERFECT JOB

A guide to discovering your gifts, following your passions, and loving your work for the rest of your life.

ROBERT BITTNER

SHAW BOOKS
an imprint of WaterBrook Press

Your Perfect Job
A SHAW BOOK
PUBLISHED BY WATERBROOK PRESS
12265 Oracle Boulevard, Suite 200
Colorado Springs, Colorado 80921

ISBN 978-0-87788-022-6

Published in the United States by WaterBrook Multnomah, an imprint of the Crown Publishing Group, a division of Random House Inc., New York.

Library of Congress Cataloging-in-Publication Data
Bittner, Robert, 1961–
    Your perfect job : a guide to discovering your gifts, following your passions, and loving your work for the rest of your life / Robert Bittner.
        p. cm.
Includes bibliographical references.
ISBN 0-87788-022-0
    1. Career development. 2. Vocational guidance. I. Title.
HF5381 .B446 2003
650.1—dc21
                                                                        2002015564

146484122

In memory of my father,
Madison R. Bittner,
who, every day, showed me what it means
to love what you do for a living.

Contents

Part 1

Where Do You Want to Go?

Chapter 1

Getting from Where You Are to Where You Want to Be

"So what are you gonna do now?"

It should be exciting when someone asks you that, because in a lot of ways, "what you're going to do now" is up to you. Your choice. I realize that may not be a lot of help if the best response you can come up with at this point is to glance away and mumble something noncommittal like, "Uhhhh-hhnnn…" But knowing you've got a choice can be an important first step if talk about careers and jobs leaves you feeling stuck, a little confused, or even terrified about moving toward doing what you really want to do. And "what you really want to do" is going to change as you learn new things, meet new people, and discover untapped interests within yourself.

Odds are good that you'll hold at least two vastly different careers over the course of your life. Plus, you'll probably change jobs numerous times as companies come and go and as your lifestyle needs change. The jobs you take and the work you do can, of course, be left up to career counselors who will steer you where they think you should go. Or you might be able to get a job by mass-mailing résumés or e-mailing all of your friends and accepting the first offer that comes along. And yes, the bills would get paid, and you'll be able to keep eating…which is nice.

But I believe there's something a whole lot better in store for you.

I believe you can get from where you are now to where you'd love to be, doing work that brings you real pleasure. Work that feels more like fun, that taps into your deepest passions and takes advantage of your skills and interests.

Maybe you know exactly what that kind of work would look like. Maybe you don't have a clue. Doesn't matter. Wherever you are—wherever you're headed—you can discover and thrive in the work you were born to do. Your perfect job.

Base Your Future on Old Movie Quotes!

Believe it or not, there's some valuable career advice buried in old movies. For the sake of argument, let's call any film before 1980 an "old movie." That way, if your parents happen to pick up this book and flip through it, they'll say, "This guy's calling *Star Wars* an old movie! Like anything made before digital effects is 'old'! What an idiot!" Then they'll throw down the book and let you get back to reading it. However, if they actually take the time to read this paragraph, they'll

---

The "Hot Jobs" Sweet Sixteen

According to the Bureau of Labor Statistics, the following jobs will be growing the most between now and 2010. In heat-index order (hottest first):[1]

1. Teachers (K–12)
2. Computer-software engineers
3. Registered nurses
4. Truck drivers
5. Computer-support specialists
6. Accountants/auditors
7. Marketing/sales managers
8. Auto mechanics
9. Health therapists
10. Police/sheriff's officers
11. Social workers
12. Engineers
13. Lawyers
14. Electricians
15. Recreation/fitness workers
16. Sales representatives

pretty much be on to my cunning plan. In that case, you'll have to wrestle them for it, because it's a lot more fun than that career book about parachutes.

But I digress.

I have two favorite movie quotes that offer stellar advice about how to choose (or not choose) a career. The first is from *Citizen Kane*. Yes, you've probably heard that critics call it one of the best (if not *the* best) American movie ever made. I happen to agree. True, nothing explodes, there's no love story to speak of, and it's in black and white. If you haven't seen it, rent it and judge for yourself. And if you'd like a tiny bit of career advice, watch for the scene between the unnamed reporter and a man named Mr. Bernstein. The reporter is in Bernstein's office, asking about the rise and fall of Bernstein's former boss, Charles Foster Kane. The reporter is a little awed by Kane's huge fortune. Mr. Bernstein, someone who knew what Kane was really like, isn't so impressed. "It isn't hard to make a lot of money," Bernstein says, "if all you want is to make a lot of money."

Whatever you can do, or dream you can, begin it. Boldness has genius, power, and magic in it.

—Johann Wolfgang von Goethe

Think about that: "It isn't hard to make a lot of money, if *all you want* is to make a lot of money." Obviously, cash flow is important. But the fact that you're reading this book makes me think making a lot of money is not *all* you want. You're probably also interested in enjoying what you do for a living, giving your talents a workout, and having time to spend with friends and family. Maybe you'd like to help others if you can or have a career that enriches your spiritual life and has meaning that stretches beyond the forty-hour workweek. In *Citizen Kane,* you could argue that Kane at one time or another sacrificed all those things. For nearly all of his life, his sole goal was to make more money so he could, as he says, "buy things."

Charles Foster Kane, you might guess, was not a happy guy.

That brings me to my *First Rule of Careers.* (There are only two. No quiz.)

The key to a great career is to love your work.

There are thousands of jobs out there. Some pay outrageously well. Some will knock the knickers off your friends when you brag about them at class reunions. Some will gain you instant respect at parties, while others will sound so complex they'll require a three-minute description of what exactly you do all day, as well as a business card, a PowerPoint presentation, and an explanatory note from your mother. But everything really boils down to this: If you don't love what you're doing, you're not going to be happy. And happiness cannot be overrated.

"I Was Not Built to Be a Hired Gun!"

After going to law school, practicing law was a bit of a shock to me. My education in no way prepared me for the actual practice of law, and I felt adrift, without any clear-cut answers or experience. It was a very frustrating time for me, very stressful. Mostly I hated it. But I did learn to grit my teeth and do things that were difficult, unfamiliar, or just plain awful.

I focused my practice on family law and soon found that I enjoyed representing children in family court. I particularly liked it because it was more than just legal representation. I acted almost like a social worker, helping families find solutions to the problems that brought them to court. Gradually I came to see that I was not built to be a hired gun and was more interested in helping people find solutions.

—BRETTE MCWHORTER SEMBER

Now, about that second movie.

If "Rosebud" is the most famous one-word line from a 1940s movie (*Citizen Kane* again), then "Plastics" has to be a contender for the most famous one-word line from a 1960s movie. It's offered to Dustin Hoffman's young character in *The Graduate* by an older family friend who just *knows* he's giving this kid the inside track to a stable, lifelong business career. Wanna be set? Easy: plastics. (It's not clear what kind of plastics the guy is talking about. Probably not Tupperware.)

The problem is, Dustin Hoffman's character couldn't care less about plastics. He's fresh out of school, a little dazed at the whole idea of having to get a job at all. He doesn't know what he wants to do with his life. But he does know that "plastics" ain't it.

And so we come to the *Second Rule of Careers*.

Finding work that you love means following your interests, abilities, and gifts.

If you love plastics, great. But if you love working with animals, measuring rainfall, making mechanical things with your hands—love any of 1,001 other things—you owe it to yourself to see where those passions can take you. And keep your eyes open: Where your personal passions lead may not always be so obvious.

FOLLOWING YOUR PASSION

Rebecca Miles Risser majored in music at a small Christian college in suburban Chicago, planning and training to make her living as a professional opera singer. After graduation she was able to get a job in the development office of the Lyric Opera of Chicago. She wasn't on stage yet, but she was a lot closer than most. In the meantime, she did as much singing on the side as possible, waiting for and working toward her big break. But the breaks just weren't coming. She was auditioning like crazy and being rejected like crazy. Rebecca had to face a hard fact.

"I came to the conclusion that I needed to reassess my goals and achievements," she says. "Given my age and experience, I realized I wouldn't be able to achieve my goals."

It can be devastating to learn that something you thought you wanted so much isn't going to happen. It's right in front of you. You can get close. But you just can't reach it.

Instead of giving up and settling for a career in the development office—or turning her back on vocal work altogether—Rebecca decided to see what things she *could* do with her interests and training. "I did some research and took a Strong Interest Survey through my former college's job placement office," she says. (The Strong Interest Survey is an instrument used by career counselors to inventory a person's interests and compare them to the job requirements of a variety of professions.) "It showed that I scored highest in the field of speech-language pathology, with 'advertising executive' coming in second." (Hmm. Sounds like a guy I heard of who was torn between going into massage therapy or heating/air-conditioning repair.)

You can have anything you want if you want it desperately enough. You must want it with an inner exuberance that erupts through the skin and joins the energy that created the world.

—SHEILA GRAHAM

"I then found a lot of speech pathologists in the area," Rebecca says. "I interviewed them and visited them at their job sites." These in-person fact-finding missions proved especially helpful. They not only helped Rebecca gain an informal understanding of the job, they also introduced her to working professionals who offered valuable advice. "People told me, 'If you're interested in voice, *this* is the school you need to go to.'" They also confirmed that she was focusing on an up-and-coming specialty. Those discussions led her to pursue a master's degree in speech pathology at Indiana University.

When we spoke, Rebecca was on staff at an Indianapolis trauma hospital, where she spends her days working with patients who are recovering from stroke, waking up from coma, and confronting complications from surgery that result in a changed mental state. She has even worked with people who have attempted suicide by shooting themselves in the head. She works to help them improve their swallowing, communication, cognitive function, voice quality, intelligibility, and language. It's a challenging job that requires a significant investment of time. "I'm seeing twenty-five to thirty-five patients at any one time," she says, adding that she typically visits each patient three to five times a week for half an hour at a time. Do the math and you'll understand why she puts in a lot of overtime.

But that's just fine with Rebecca. It's work that many find unbearably draining both emotionally and physically, but she's thriving. "My spiritual gifts happen to be intercession, mercy, and compassion," she says. "That's a strong combination to apply in a hospital setting. I do feel that I am offering something special to people. I'm meeting unique needs in a unique way. I have a real passion for what I'm doing."

From opera singer to speech pathologist. Sounds like somebody whose career took a wrong turn somewhere. But in fact, it's just the opposite: a person who found a fulfilling new way to live out her deepest career goals. The elements of singing that most appealed to Rebecca—the nuts-and-bolts mechanics of using the voice to communicate—are still the focus of her work. In addition, she is now able to do much more than entertain. She's able to help people regain their ability to speak.

IN SEARCH OF THE PERFECT JOB

Rebecca has found her perfect job. I'm another one of those rare, weird people who can say the same thing: I love what I do for a living. So when a local teacher read an article of mine in a national magazine and invited me to speak to her high-school class about being a writer, I jumped at the chance. I love talking with people about being a writer. And now I had the chance to inspire a New Generation to follow in my brave footsteps.

Well actually, what went through my mind was: "High-school kids. Cool."

Turns out, though, that her "high-school" class wasn't held at the high school at all. In fact, it was part of an educational program at Michigan's Eaton County Youth Services, a maximum-security juvenile detention center.

The one-story Youth Services building is a low-slung, plain-looking brick structure at the very end of a dead-end road. (I'm sure that doesn't send any of these kids the wrong message.) To get in, I signed a book at the front desk and then waited to get buzzed through two locked and guarded doors. After that I was accompanied at all times by another adult. And when the kids themselves moved from room to room, they had to pass single file through the halls, in silent groups of five or six, a stern adult chaperone eyeing them every step of the way. Other than that, it was pretty much your typical high-school English class: a balanced mix of guys and girls—some bored, some enthusiastic—ranging in age from about fifteen to seventeen.

After introducing myself, I gave them a quick look at my typical workday:

I'm usually out of bed by 6:00 A.M. By 7:30 or 8:00 I'm at the computer with a cup of coffee, checking my e-mail and going over my to-do list for the day. If I don't have any urgent deadlines, I'll read the newspaper or surf the Internet for story ideas and write them up as article proposals, which I then e-mail to the magazines that are likely to be interested. Often, I'll need to do some telephone interviews or other research for articles I'm already working on. I also spend a fair amount of time networking with other freelancers through online discussion lists and e-mail.

Yeah, and some days I actually write.

I hit my stride and went on to tell them about the incredible flexibility I have as a self-employed, work-at-home guy. If I need to run a personal errand during the day (that is, if I run out of coffee and start shaking), I can do that without ticking anybody off. If my work is in good shape, I can even catch an early-afternoon movie in the middle of the week. (That's rare, though. No, really.) How I spend my days—from the hours I work to the topics I write about—is, for the most part, entirely up to me.

What a shock: These kids *loved* the idea of being a freelance writer! No boss. No set schedule. The freedom to spend your days doing what you want to do, how you want to do it. It's a pretty attractive lifestyle for most people. (Well, *duh*.) But c'mon. Who *wouldn't* like to be able to take off early on a Tuesday afternoon and catch a movie, hit the mall, visit the zoo, or spend a couple hours having coffee with your self-employed (or, um, unemployed) friends?

But wait a second. Yeah, my job has its advantages. But just like being a

---

"I Never Knew This Was a Career!"

I have a very strong food background—a bachelor's degree in foods and nutrition and a master's in food and business. My first job out of college was in a test kitchen for General Foods. I was a "test kitchen home economist." For instance, say there was a new flavor of Jell-O pudding. I would work on package directions, come up with recipes using the product, and then present it to the ad agency. I was exposed to recipe development, package photography, and product advertising—all of which tie together. As soon as I discovered product photography, it was like falling into a stream. I was a natural for it. I took it for granted what food should look like, but I never knew it was a career called food stylist. I've been doing food styling exclusively for nineteen years.

—CAROL SMOLER

chemistry teacher, an architect, a graphic designer, a computer-game programmer, an electrician, or a car dealer, writing is also a job. It's a job that I love, but it's still a job. And like every job, it's got a downside.

Instead of having one boss, I have a different boss for just about everything I write. Editors request (that is, demand) changes to something I thought was perfect when I turned it in. Revisions are a basic fact of life. So is the rejection of story ideas I've spent hours developing. Deadlines must be met, no matter what—which means that sometimes I have sixteen-hour workdays and Saturday and Sunday workdays. I don't get paid if I don't work because I feel sick or I'd like to take two weeks' vacation or there's a *Buffy* marathon on TV. Unreturned phone calls, unfair contracts, days when you just don't feel like writing, paychecks that should have arrived four weeks ago. They're all part of the wonderful freelance writing life.

And why not? Every job has its ups and downs. Every job is going to involve things you love doing and things that make you question your sanity. That's all right. The secret is finding the job you love so much—that is so personally rewarding—that the upside outweighs the downside.

If you think "The Perfect Job" won't involve headaches, problems, challenges, and occasionally grumpy bosses, then I'm afraid you're going to have a long and very frustrating search. I don't believe there's One Perfect Job for everyone.

What I do believe is this: When it comes to work, I don't think anything is better than spending your days doing exactly what you know you were created to do. And the rewards are not only internal and personal. People who love what they're doing are more likely to be better at their jobs than people who are simply going through the motions—and that applies whether you're discovering a new star or flipping a better burger. If you love what you do for a living, everybody wins.

But maybe you don't buy it. Maybe you know people who are dragging themselves through the workweek just so they can cut loose and party on the weekend. People who hate to face Monday morning because it means another five days stuck in a job they can't stand. Classmates who couldn't care less about school because they have no idea where it's going to take them. The workaholics who log sixty to seventy hours on the job every week because they're striving for "something better."

Maybe you know people who see work as nothing more than a solid, dependable way to keep gas in the car and cable on the TV. Or maybe you yourself are struggling and frustrated with work, wondering how you can possibly be expected to know, at seventeen or nineteen or twenty-five or whatever, what One Big Thing you're supposed to be doing with your life. How can you make a choice without second-guessing your decision, wondering if you just made the biggest mistake of your life?

The Not-So-Hot Jobs of the Future

The Bureau of Labor Statistics has pinpointed sixteen jobs that will either show the least amount of growth or the largest expected losses between now and 2010. Does that mean you shouldn't pursue number fourteen—funeral director—if that's what you want to do? Not at all. If that's your passion, do it; there's certainly a need. In fact, you'll face less competition and might be able to rise to the top faster. But know going in that you *might* face some rougher-than-normal economic slumps along the way. So, with the least-promising jobs first:

1. Farmers/ranchers
2. Phone-switchboard operators
3. Bank tellers
4. Insurance claims clerks
5. Word processors/typists
6. Sewing-machine operators
7. Butchers
8. Meter readers
9. Parts salespeople
10. Procurement clerks
11. Movie projectionists
12. Proofreaders
13. Loggers
14. Funeral directors
15. Insurance underwriters
16. Travel agents

This book will help.

In the following chapters you'll find story after story of how real people coped with the challenges of finding a rewarding job and making it in the workplace. They'll tell you how they made the most of their first job, overcame on-the-job hurdles to success, followed their changing interests, grew in their careers, and meshed their deepest beliefs with their daily work.

We'll also look at finding the job or, better yet, *jobs* that are right for your unique blend of interests, talents, and abilities—and figuring out just what those interests, talents, and abilities are. That's the only way you're going to find true joy in work. By nailing down your interests, talents, and abilities, you'll be better equipped to move past just holding a job and start building a productive career that will help you become the person God truly wants you to be.

Finally, you'll get the information you need to really thrive in your career—from handling missteps and setbacks to living out your faith in the workplace and taking inventory of your job situation. After all, the job that was right for you two years ago may not be right today, with your newly acquired skills, life experiences, and interests. Maybe the job that fit perfectly when you were single or childless just isn't compatible anymore with a life that includes a spouse or children. Changes in location, education, marital status, and lifestyle affect the kind of job that fits you at any given time. We'll look at whether you are maxing out your abilities and skills in light of your current situation.

There's a TV commercial I see every now and then that features a way-enthusiastic man promoting his book on government grants that anybody can apply for. "The government will pay you to write your novel!" he claims. "Want to start your own business? The government has money to help!" With the help of these grants, this man assures us, you won't have to be tied down to a life that you loathe. You'll have the freedom to do what you really want to do in life. "And doing what you love for a living is like being on vacation every day of your life!!" he says.

I don't quite understand this guy's suit (it's covered with dozens of question marks, like The Riddler) or his *NOT! VERY! SUBTLE!!* sales pitch. But I think he's got one thing absolutely right: Doing what you love for a living is one of the most fulfilling and significant things you can do. Besides, it's fun.

Now "doing what you love" may not *really* be like vacation—if by "vacation" you mean doing nothing but lying on a warm beach, sipping a cool beverage, and working on your tan. (Hey, even swimsuit models don't have it so easy.) But if "vacation" means spending your days doing something you really enjoy, having moments when you smack yourself on the forehead and think, "Wow, I can't believe I'm really *here*. I can't believe I'm really *doing* this"…well, then, I believe that doing your perfect job really *can* be a lot like vacation. And you won't even lose your luggage.

Are you ready?

Chapter 2

Get Passionate!

I'm passionate about my job. I think you can be too. In fact, I think it's one of the keys to building a successful and satisfying career.

So what's the big deal about passion? Let's break down what happens if "career" just means a job or jobs that pay the bills.

Say you decide to be a plumber. Obviously a great way to earn a living. You can set your own hours, earn good money, and provide services and skills that the average person can't duplicate without spraying water—or something worse—everywhere. Maybe you even enjoy it enough to work free for your family and friends, just because you love the heft of a pipe wrench and the satisfaction that comes from solving problems with your hands.

But suppose you slide out of bed some Monday down the road, and you suddenly realize that you'd rather eat newspaper than deal with one more plugged toilet or clogged garbage disposal. What job options do you really have? Plumbing is what you do; being a plumber is all you know. So you sigh, drag yourself into your work clothes, set your jaw, and tell yourself that you have no choice but to suck it up and carry on. Plumbing is all you've got. It used to be fun. Now it's work. And you're suddenly feeling trapped like a glob of hair in a U-joint...and a little desperate.

Now instead, imagine building your career around your passion. While plumbing might reflect one aspect of what you really love doing—solving problems by working with your hands, say—there are tons of other jobs that can develop out of that original passion. If the plumbing competition gets too stiff or some genius invents maintenance-free pipes, you'll still be able to live out your passion and have a fulfilling career by shifting to some other work that requires you to solve problems by working with your hands.

Some people think ideas like "following your passion" are only for creative types or for "losers" who can't get real jobs. These people think "passion" sounds too intangible and undependable. "You're better off just finding a good job and sticking with it," they say.

But that's the problem.

In today's workplace, there are no employment guarantees. The old model of the worker who hires on at a company straight out of high school or college and stays with that company straight through to retirement is long gone. In today's business world, "change" is the mantra, and those changes usually are not in the employee's best interest. Companies routinely downsize and restructure, laying off hundreds—if not thousands—of workers at a time. For those who remain, the pace of work is faster than ever before, and the pressure to "produce" just builds and builds. For many, there's never any escape. Thanks to cell phones, e-mail, instant messaging, wireless communication, and home offices, a lot of people are finding themselves on-call 24/7.

Given the state of today's workplace, if you're not passionate about what you're doing, you'll likely burn out or turn cynical. And you won't be the only one paying the price. Your job stress is bound to affect family and friends—not to mention the quality of your work. By contrast, following your passion

---

The U.S. Immigration and Naturalization Service wants to hire thousands of new border-patrol guards and immigration inspectors to process and keep better track of new arrivals. These positions require just a high-school diploma. With overtime, the jobs can pay around $40,000 the first year.

actually leads to a greater sense of personal fulfillment, enriching you as an individual and as a member of a larger community.

People with Passion

When it comes to finding a job you can love, the Bible offers several general, helpful guidelines. Consider these verses:

Love the Lord your God with all your heart and with all your soul and with all your mind. (Matthew 22:37)

Love your neighbor as yourself. (Matthew 22:39)

Go into all the world and preach the good news to all creation. (Mark 16:15)

Whatever you do, work at it with all your heart, as working for the Lord, not for men, since you know that you will receive an inheritance from the Lord as a reward. It is the Lord Christ you are serving. (Colossians 3:23-24)

Each of these essentials helps guide and direct us as we try to figure out and follow God's will for our lives. On one hand, they will lead us *away from* jobs and career goals that simply don't fit with living a moral, biblically based life. (After all, it's kind of hard to reconcile being a nude dancer or a mob hit man with a commitment to following what Jesus taught.) On the other hand, these essentials help lead us *toward* those activities and attitudes that will fulfill us as human beings and bring glory to our Creator. All sorts of motivational and self-help books and speakers will talk about "following your bliss," discovering your purpose in life, and making a living by doing what you love. But I believe that it's only when we go after those ideals from the foundation of Christian faith that our efforts will yield anything worth holding on to.

Before we go any further, though, I think it's important to look at two myths that have arisen about Christians and work.

Myth No. 1: Only Professional Ministers Are "Called" to a Specific Career

I come from a family of professional ministers. My father was a minister, as was his father; one uncle and aunt were missionaries to Bolivia; another uncle and aunt were missionaries in France and Belgium for forty years; and I have cousins who are missionaries in Europe and Canada. Because of my family's close connection with the "professional ministry," I spent much of my teen years believing that "calling" was something experienced by only a select, holy few.

Climb high

Climb far

Your goal the sky

Your aim the star.

—INSCRIPTION AT WILLIAMS COLLEGE, WILLIAMSTOWN, MASSACHUSETTS

At the risk of offending my fellow college alumni, I realized how crazy that idea was when I saw a lot of my former Christian-college classmates become professional ministers. I mean, I *knew* these people. They were the same people who set off smoke bombs in the dorms, made prank phone calls at midnight, and broke the campus curfew to go out for a postmidnight snack. (Wait a second. That last one was me.) I loved them and cherished their friendship. But thinking of them as "holy" or "perfect"? Not gonna happen.

And yet today many of them are pastors, missionaries, and church leaders. They are obviously where they're supposed to be, doing what they're supposed to be doing. My conclusion: Professional ministers—from choir directors to children's ministers to youth workers to pastors—are human beings just like the rest of us. Sure, they're "called." But so are the rest of us.

In her essay "Why Work?" theologian, mystery writer, and playwright (there's a person who wasn't afraid to explore a variety of passions) Dorothy L. Sayers wrote,

> Christian people…must get it firmly into their heads that when a man or woman is called to a particular job of secular work, that is as true a vocation as though he or she were called to specifically religious work.[1]

Or, as my father liked to say, "We are all ministers." And the ministry really begins, I believe, when we find the courage to follow our passions into the workplace.

Professional ministers talk openly about "hearing God's call" for their lives. So should we. There's nothing shameful or embarrassing about saying we have a calling. And the validity of our calling doesn't hang on whether we spend our days keeping machinery running smoothly, serving customers well, counseling single mothers, performing brain surgery, or writing jokes for cereal boxes.

Myth No. 2: Our "Calling" or "Career Passion" Is God's Little Secret

Too many Christians accept as fact the myth that God doesn't want us to know what he is calling us to do. As a result, they become increasingly frustrated when their pleas to God for guidance go unanswered. They want more than anything to do what God wants them to do, but they hear no specific heavenly leading. Their every effort to somehow unlock God's best for them leads to frustration.

God is not a great cosmic safe in which the answers to all of our questions are stored—if only we can figure out the right combination. He did not create us with a specific job to do and then decide to play hide-and-seek with the information. Throughout the Bible, God makes plain his desires for his people. He doesn't leave them guessing. He is not stingy with answers, and he isn't frugal in meeting his people's needs. Instead, he speaks to them—sometimes audibly on his own, sometimes through others, and sometimes through signs, experiences, and circumstances. Moses and Samuel heard God's own voice. Peter, James, and John heard the call from Jesus' lips. Later, on the Day of Pentecost, a group of believers experienced the Holy Spirit's call through extraordinary sights and sounds. Both Jonah and Paul had life-altering "experiences." Whether it was through the Urim and Thummim (ancient tools used to determine God's will), drawing lots, asking for a specific answer to prayer, seeing visions, being visited by angels, or killing time in a fish's digestive tract, the people of the Bible knew what it was that God

---

"Hey, Baby!"

My first postcollege, full-time job was managing a maternity store, which—as odd as that was for an unmarried, no-kids twenty-two-year-old—was something I loved. I was working there part time during my senior year of college; after college, the owners offered me full-time management. Seemed like a good choice for an English major who didn't want to teach! I did it for two years. I loved it because it was so service-oriented. Women weren't just buying clothes; they needed help coping with pregnancy, self-image, unexpected problems, et cetera. Because the store was a small boutique, it didn't offer any further career options. I thought about regular retail, but I really didn't want to give up the more specialized kind of work I was doing. Eventually, I left to become a travel agent.

—AMY REA

wanted them to do. Although the avenues for discerning God's call may be different for us today, God's love and care for his people remain unchanged.

I know people who worry themselves silly wondering if what they most want to do is what God wants them to do. Well, to be honest, I'm not convinced that God really cares whether I am a secular recording artist, a neuroscientist, a park ranger, or a postal worker. What God cares about is how we glorify him by being living examples of his love among the people of this world. "Work is not, primarily, a thing one does to live," Dorothy Sayers wrote, "but the thing one lives to do. It is, or it should be, the full expression of the worker's faculties, the thing in which he finds spiritual, mental, and bodily satisfaction, and the medium in which he offers himself to God."[2] We'll discuss this in more detail in chapter 4, but for now, I'll boil it down to this: Through your gifts, talents, and natural interests, God has already given you a good idea of where you're probably best equipped to flourish as the person he made you to be. That doesn't mean the signs will always be obvious to you—if they were, you wouldn't need this book—but the raw material for where you can go and what you can be is already part of your personal makeup. When everything clicks into place—when we discover what we love doing and find interesting ways to do it—then we are in the process of living out that "full expression" Sayers is talking about. And that can't help but lead to personal fulfillment and glory to God.

SO WHAT ARE YOU PASSIONATE ABOUT?

You probably have friends who have known since elementary school what work they wanted to do when they grew up. You know, the mechanic whose parents can tell story after story about how "he's always been taking things apart and putting them back together again." The botanist who, as a child, was always rummaging in people's flower beds for "samples." The future veterinarian who always had a way with the neighborhood strays. The software designer who even as a kid preferred the company of microchips.

These are the exceptions. Not everybody knows what they want to do when they grow up—and that includes some forty-year-olds!

If you're not sure what you're really passionate about—because you enjoy doing a whole lot of things or because you can't really pinpoint any one thing yet that makes your blood race—start by asking yourself three questions:

- What activities do I enjoy?
- What am I good at?
- What have I done that felt worthwhile?

Don't be shy. Feel free to write down anything that comes to mind, and don't worry if you start to fill up a sheet of paper. The more thoughts you have, the more choices and options you have. As you answer these questions, consider the following points.

What Activities Do I Enjoy?

This is not the place to self-censor. If you love to play video games, watch TV for hours at a time, or experiment with various shades of lip gloss, write it down. If you love reading thick fantasy novels, write it down. If your dream of sheer bliss is to pack a room with friends and crank up the volume on Gwen Stefani, write it down. If you like to cook, work on your car, skateboard, play the bassoon, create your own graphic novels, or search for music files on the Internet...you guessed it: Write it down. Turn off the little voice that's telling you, "Nobody cares about *that*," or "There's no way *that* could be a career!"

Need help? Here are ten things from my list:

1. watching lots of TV
2. collecting movies on tape and disc
3. reading magazines
4. eating/drinking
5. spending time with animals
6. traveling
7. listening to music

8. playing musical instruments

9. playing with computers/electronic gadgets

10. surfing the Web

Of course, this probably explains why the Nobel Prize committee hasn't called me yet, but you get the idea.

What Am I Good At?

Since we'll be talking about practical skills in chapter 3, try to focus your answers here on those things that come naturally to you as a person—your natural gifts and talents, not skills that can be learned. For instance, maybe you've discovered that you can pick up foreign languages pretty easily or that you seem to have a great aptitude for math. Or maybe you're a good listener or someone who can help others think through complicated life issues. Maybe you can help people relax with your sense of humor or you're great at comforting people in pain.

Chances are this question is going to be a bit harder to answer—not because you aren't good at many things, but because we aren't used to thinking about ourselves in these terms. If we can play the drums, guitar, and piano, it may amaze the folks next door but not seem like any big deal to us. We take such gifts for granted. ("What? Can't everybody play two keyboards at the same time?") So take time to really think about your own unique mix of talents. List as many as you can, but don't stop until you have at least five.

What Have I Done That Felt Worthwhile?

This is where you list those activities that strike a chord inside of you, bringing a deeper sense of satisfaction than what you'd experience from simply doing a job well or doing something that was just fun.

Some of these activities might have come out of volunteer jobs you've held: delivering meals to shut-ins, leading worship services at a homeless shelter, working a suicide prevention hotline. But don't limit yourself to so-called official volunteer work. Maybe you were able to help a friend work through her emotions about a surprise pregnancy. Maybe you counseled someone who was beginning to experiment with drugs. Maybe you chose to spend time with an elderly neighbor, not because he needed your help, but simply because you enjoyed his company. Maybe you led a children's choir at church or helped a retarded adult put a puzzle together.

Whatever. Write down anything you've done that touched your heart and made you feel as if you were playing an important role in someone else's life.

Looking for Patterns

Now that you've listed as many activities as you can think of, what patterns emerge? To see them, try to look beneath the surface.

If you don't know where you're going, you will probably end up somewhere else.
—LAURENCE JOHNSTON PETER

Maybe you enjoy playing classical guitar, and you're actually good at it. Does that mean you should start planning a world tour or move to the nearest music capital? Not necessarily. Take the time to ask yourself what you *really* find most fulfilling about playing the guitar. Is it the meter and structure of the music itself? the historical connection you feel between yourself and composers of two hundred years ago? the feeling of control that comes from manipulating an audience's emotional response? the pleasure of seeing your audience enjoy your performance? Any one of these answers could lead to dozens of different "passions"—including many that have little or nothing to do with guitar playing or even music. For instance, if you decide that you most enjoy the feeling you get when making connections between long-dead composers and present-day performance, you might be happy as a history teacher who brings the past to life for today's students.

To get a better understanding of where you could work, where you might go to school, what direction may be best for you, ask the advice of parents, coworkers, and friends. They can help you understand what things in life really excite you. If you aren't quite sure what you are passionate about—what you'd do with your life if you could do absolutely anything at all—ask these people what they see in you that you might be missing.

Also discuss your situation with a guidance or career counselor. They are trained professionals who have dozens of personal assessment tools and surveys that ferret out interests you didn't realize you had and point you to the particular jobs that match.

The construction industry needs almost a quarter of a million new workers each year. (Because of retirement, not accidents!) Top construction workers—plumbers, electricians, carpenters, bricklayers, roofers, and painters—can earn more than $100,000 a year.

Once you have a lead on several directions that interest you, follow up at the library, on the Internet, and through personal interviews with professionals actively involved in those jobs. Don't be shy. Most people get so used to the daily routine of their jobs that they can easily become blasé about what they do for a living. But show up on their doorstep curious and enthusiastic, and you'll quickly learn whether or not they're passionate about what they do—and whether you could be too.

Finally, and most important, pray that God will lead you in the right direction.

Get to Know Yourself

To get a better idea of your own skills, abilities, and interests, ask a guidance or career counselor about the following testing tools:

- *Meyers-Briggs Type Indicator*—A good starting point for learning more about your own personality and interests.
- *Strong Interest Survey*—Explores a range of possible careers, including new options you might never have previously considered, based on information supplied by experienced professionals already active in a variety of jobs.
- *Campbell Interest and Skill Survey*—Primarily for the college-bound, this survey measures your interest in a variety of jobs as well as your confidence in your ability to perform various job-related skills.

What You Do and Who You Are

I recently read a statement posted on a Web site in which the writer said, "Trying to determine what God wants you to do with your life is extremely tough. (That's an understatement!)" I think this writer found it so tough because he was going at it backwards. He wanted to know God's will before he took his first step.

God is concerned more with who we are as people and what we accomplish for his kingdom than what company we work for or what our title is. Remember Colossians 3:23-24:

> Whatever you do, work at it with all your heart, as working for the
> Lord, not for men, since you know that you will receive an inheritance
> from the Lord as a reward. It is the Lord Christ you are serving.

Or, as Rebecca Miles Risser told me during one of our conversations, "The question is: Who are you going to become by doing what you do?"

After my wife and I signed the initial paperwork to buy our first new car, we were ushered into the den of the credit manager. The man was like human electricity, talking nonstop as he keyed our information into his computer, zoomed his chair back and forth between desk and printer, and dealt out a growing collection of documents for our signatures. I think he also answered several phone calls and a page from the public-address system. It was after nine o'clock at night and the man was a blur of frenzied motion. He told us this was pretty much how he spent every working hour. "My wife hates my schedule," he said, "but, hey, I just tell her that we'll be able to retire in style by the time I'm forty." *Yeah,* I remember thinking, *if you're lucky enough to live that long. And if she hasn't packed up and left you by then.*

I have no idea what this man's relationship with God was. But I feel fairly safe in saying that God probably didn't intend for him to sacrifice family and possibly health for the sake of an early retirement. I think it's probably safe to say that his job was helping him become someone *less* than he could be.

Bible translator Duane Clouse, based in Irian Jaya, Indonesia, offers a contrasting experience:

> I love my work because it is so varied. One moment I'm a literacy teacher or a mechanic, carpenter, or plumber. Sometimes I'm an ethno-musicologist, linguist, anthropologist, and, if everything goes right, I can be a Bible translator, too! But my real work is to *personally* be a translation to people who have never heard of God.

I can't say this any plainer: Life is just too short to be doing work that makes you miserable or bores you or turns you away from God. If you're going to be doing any work at all, you might as well be doing something you're really passionate about, something worthwhile that's going to count for something in the world.

Because that's where the joy is.

Chapter 3

Taking Stock of Your Skills

When I was just beginning to make plans to leave my day job and become self-employed, I signed up for a one-day seminar on How to Manage Your Home-Based Business. On a Thursday morning, about a dozen independent-minded folks like me met in a conference room at the local mall, eager to soak up whatever information the speaker could provide.

The occupations people wanted to pursue out of their homes ranged from graphic designer to plumber to lawyer. I was surprised to be the only writer. (I thought everybody wanted to be a writer…) But I was even more surprised that some of the people at the seminar didn't know what they wanted to do or what they were capable of doing. They just knew, deep down, that they wanted to work for themselves. And most of them were frustrated because they didn't believe there was anything they were qualified to do. They felt their desires were running headlong into the brick wall of their limited skills.

Or rather, their *perceived* limited skills. The leader, Barbara, didn't have to ask too many questions to figure out that these people had more going for them than they had first thought.

Barbara turned to a young woman, a recent college grad, who was living at home and working part time at Wal-Mart while she tried to figure out where she really wanted to go in life. "What do you enjoy most about your job?" Barbara asked.

The young woman thought a moment. "Well, all of my friends think it's really weird, but I actually enjoy 'zoning.'"

"Zoning?"

"Yeah, I work in ladies wear, and 'zoning' is when we pick up all of the stuff that people have just dropped on the floor or left in the changing rooms and put it back in the right place on the sales floor."

"You mean hanging stuff up?"

"It's more than that. On the racks, everything's grouped by color, then by pattern, then by size. And you wouldn't believe how much clothing people can scatter around. It's actually a lot of work."

Barbara paused. "So it sounds like you enjoy bringing order out of chaos. And you don't mind hard work. What did you study in school?"

The young woman shrugged. "Well…business management. I thought that might help me figure out where I want to go, but it didn't work out that way."

Blessed is he who has found his work; let him ask no other blessedness.

—THOMAS CARLYLE

"Okay, you've got a basic business foundation, then. So actually—I'm sorry, what's your name?"

"Meghan."

"Actually, Meghan, I think there's a ton of things you could be successful at that tie into your interests and your education. You might want to consider starting your own home-and-office cleaning company. Or interior decorating. Or becoming a consultant focusing on organization techniques for people with cluttered closets. You might laugh"—and some did—"but nowadays that's a multimillion-dollar industry. People don't have time to do a lot of their own…um…'zoning' these days, so they're happy to pay experts who can handle it for them."

Suddenly Meghan sat up and smiled. For the first time she could see the possibilities.

From Mozart to Michael Jackson

Maybe you've heard of some of the following people:

- *Wolfgang Amadeus Mozart* was four years old when he went on a concert tour of Europe, astounding audiences with his musical skills on the harpsichord, violin, and organ.
- *Jodie Foster* made her movie debut at ten in the Disney film *Napoleon and Samantha.*
- *Michael Jackson* was around four when he started singing with his brothers in the Jackson Five.
- *Ron Howard,* the film director of *Backdraft, Apollo 13, EdTV,* and *A Beautiful Mind,* first rose to fame as a seven-year-old in television's *The Andy Griffith Show.*
- *Jennifer Capriati* was fourteen when she began playing—and winning—major tennis matches.
- *Homer Hickam,* now a retired NASA engineer, started shooting off homemade rockets when he was just a teenager.

And as you're reading this, there are probably hundreds of other child wonders out there who are mixing things in test tubes, practicing scales, discovering comets, creating a faster network for their home computers, developing recipes, cultivating rare orchids, and dissecting dead birds. It's as if they're born knowing exactly what they want to do for the rest of their lives.

They're not like the rest of us. That's okay. For most of us, it takes time to grow into our talents and figure out exactly where we want to invest our energy.

One of the stumbling blocks along the way is this: Most of us lump *skills* and *abilities* in the same category, throwing *gifts* and *talents* into the mix for good measure. It's helpful to make some distinctions between these words, though.

A *gift* or *talent* is a natural, God-given ability that you were born with. Thank your parents' genes.

A *skill* is an ability based on knowledge and expertise that you have learned. Thank your teachers.

Even so, it isn't simply a matter of being born with a talent or not. There are prodigies who can master chess at the age of six; that's a gift. But it doesn't mean the rest of us are incapable of playing the game. Practically everyone of average mental capacity can learn to play chess. So while natural gifts or talents can give you a head start in your career, they are more like a building block for your future rather than the entire skyscraper.

The Fair Labor Standards Act states that employers are not required to pay tipped employees more than $2.13 an hour in wages. *However*, if the sum of tips plus $2.13 an hour falls below the minimum wage, the employer is required by law to make up the difference.

Skills are learned abilities that often develop out of the interests that arise as a result of our gifts. Confusing? Think of it this way. To be a successful interior designer, you've got to have a good eye for color, a sense of aesthetic balance, and a creative spirit. These are all things that, perhaps, can be augmented by education and training but are, primarily, natural gifts. If someone can't tell chartreuse from teal, no amount of training is going to help. What *will* help, though, is an education in decorating that teaches a designer to bring her sense of color, balance, and creativity together in fabrics, paint, furniture, and decorative details that will establish the right atmosphere for a specific space and client. (If you think that sounds easy, catch a couple episodes of The Learning Channel's *Trading Spaces* or BBC America's *Changing Rooms*.)

If you don't know exactly what your skills are or don't feel pulled in a specific career direction based on your natural talents and abilities, this chapter will help.

DISCOVERING WHAT YOU CAN DO

Ask most people to make a list of their skills, and they'll probably stare at you blankly. Or at best, come up with one or two ideas such as: "I'm good at fixing things," or "I really like working with kids." Because most people, when they think about their own unique skills and the roles those skills might play in their career, think along the lines of "Well, I don't really have any important skills," or "Nobody's looking to hire somebody who does *that*."

You may not yet be able to recognize the skills you use every day. But that doesn't mean you don't have any or that your skills are not valuable. To get a better handle on your skills, consider the following self-assessment approaches.

Analyze Your Accomplishments

In the *K.I.S.S. Guide to Managing Your Career* (the *"K.I.S.S."* stands for "Keep It Simple Series"), career management counselor Ken Lawson suggests looking back over your personal life and any work experience you may already have had and identifying six to eight significant accomplishments. "There are several important guidelines for selecting each accomplishment," he writes:

- It must be the achievement of a goal that involved you directly.
- It must be something you did well for which you received some recognition: praise, awards, compliments, or even just a pat on the back.
- It must be something that made you feel proud at the time....

Next, Lawson says:

Write down as many details as you can recall about each of
the…accomplishments. Recapture the background and setting of each
accomplishment, and write about the activities you did to reach that outcome.…

For each of your accomplishments, use the following list to take
inventory of the activities you did that helped you achieve your significant accomplishments.

administering	conserving	eliminating
advising	consolidating	enforcing
analyzing	constructing	establishing
arranging	consulting	evaluating
assembling	converting	expanding
assessing	coordinating	expediting
assisting	correcting	fabricating
balancing	counseling	facilitating
budgeting	creating	forming
building	debating	founding
calculating	deciding	guiding
coaching	defining	handling
communicating	delegating	hiring
compiling	demonstrating	identifying
completing	designing	improving
composing	developing	initiating
computing	directing	innovating
condensing	discussing	inspecting
conducting	editing	installing

instructing	planning	researching
interpreting	presenting	resolving
introducing	processing	revising
inventing	producing	serving
leading	promoting	sharing
learning	protecting	showing
making	providing	staffing
managing	publicizing	streamlining
marketing	publishing	supervising
modifying	reading	teaching
motivating	recording	tending
negotiating	recruiting	testing
opening	reducing	training
operating	refining	traveling
organizing	repairing	updating
performing	reporting	upgrading[1]
persuading	representing	

Among the words that Lawson includes in his list are:

Once you've associated as many of these words as possible with your half-dozen or so accomplishments, look for patterns. You've probably used a lot of the same skills to accomplish a variety of things. Call these your frequently used skills.

Next, choose ten of the frequently used skills that mean the most to you, that you're really passionate about. Call these your motivated skills, the skills that, according to Lawson, "you must be able to perform and practice in a work setting in order to achieve congruence—an ideal fit." Also, if you are able to list your motivated skills to interviewers and your networking contacts, you'll be providing a very specific outline of the kind of positions you can excel in. (For more information about the *K.I.S.S. Guide to Managing Your Career* and other skill-assessment tools, check the resources section at the back of this book.)

"What I Learned at Hamburger High"

I started at McDonald's as a milkshake maker at eighteen and left as an assistant manager at age nineteen.

The rules seemed endless. Your uniform had to be clean, your hair had to be pinned up, your smile had to look sincere, you got docked for being even a smidgen late, idle moments were to be filled with wiping and polishing. To this day, I know how to ensure a hamburger cooks all the way through by pressing it to the grill with a spatula. I also know that customers require friendly cultivation, and that "Thank you" is a magic phrase for bringing back business.

McDonald's managers went to Hamburger High, the prep school for Hamburger University, the company's national training center. That's where we learned how to work with people.

The people-management skills are the interesting part to me now, because they are so simple, so successful, and so neglected by many businesses. Volumes have been written about people-management skills, but my Hamburger High notebook says them in three no-frills paragraphs:

Leadership. Communication skills. Organizing and planning. Self-evaluation.

Make a person want to do a good job. Satisfaction-getters are achievement, recognition, responsibility, advancement.

Set goals. Imagine the ideal situation. Listen to others. Ask questions. Read.

A lot of people think that flipping burgers at McDonald's is a lowly, no-brainer job with nothing to gain but tired feet.

They must never have done it.

—HOLLY OCASIO RIZZO

Seek Feedback

In the home-based business seminar, Meghan wasn't able to see the link between what she enjoyed doing in her part-time job and what she could do for a career until somebody pointed it out to her. She was too close to the situation. Maybe you are too. So be willing to ask others what they have seen in you that you may be overlooking.

Start with a guidance or career counselor. If you're still in school, make it a point to spend time talking with those professionals who have made a career out of helping others find a career. But be aware that many guidance counselors (especially at the high-school or junior-college level) may not have the time to really get to know you, your interests, and your aspirations. They may be used to directing students toward pat, specific paths; they may not know about all of the options available to you. They may not be able to recommend schools or companies outside your state, for instance, or they might not be up to date on the current job market. They may feel overwhelmed with application forms, test scores, and other paperwork.

So include a guidance or career counselor in your assessment mix. But do not stop there. Ask friends, relatives, coworkers, and former employers what skills and abilities they see in you. Be open to looking at yourself through their eyes.

Test Yourself

Dozens of personality, skill, and interest tests exist to help you pinpoint your passions and abilities. Some were mentioned in chapter 2. A career counselor can suggest others. One of the best tools I've found, however, is called the National Career Aptitude System (NCAS). A complete series of tests, along with about sixty pages of career descriptions, is included in the book *Discover What You're Best At* by Linda Gale.

Six separate self-scoring tests make up the NCAS, covering Business aptitude, Clerical skills, Logic, Mechanical reasoning, Numerical skill, and Social abilities. Each test will take about thirty minutes, so you'll need to set aside several hours to complete the entire system. But it will be time well spent.

After working your way through the tests and the scoring, you may find that you scored about as you expected. I know I did—scoring "low average" in Numerical, for example, when I recently test-drove the test for this book. But you may be surprised where your strong skill areas lead you. I was highest in Clerical skills, followed by Business and Logic, then Mechanical and Social. Those results suggested five main career "clusters" I could successfully pursue, depending on what I'd most like to focus on. I narrowed the field to three main clusters: Business/Clerical/Logic, Business/Clerical/Social, and Clerical/Logic/Social.

The return from your work must be the satisfaction which that work brings you and the world's need of that work. With this, life is heaven, or as near heaven as you can get. Without this—with work which you despise, which bores you, and which the world does not need—this life is hell.

—W. E. B. DuBois

The B/C/L cluster listed jobs that involve book editing (which I've done as a staff person and continue to do as a freelancer) and reporting/editing (which is basically how I make the rest of my living). That same cluster, though, also includes a variety of jobs that would never have occurred to me, including hydroponics-nursery manager, nursing-home dietitian, and quality-assurance coordinator.

The C/L/S cluster, which tied for "first-place cluster" in my mind, again included news reporter and some other jobs from the B/C/L list, but it also added interesting careers such as epidemiologist, detective, psychiatric social worker, and—*ta da!*—career-information specialist and guidance counselor. (So hey, you'd better listen up.)

It was gratifying that the tests reflect what I'd already been feeling in my heart—that I'm doing exactly what I'm supposed to be doing. But it was also really interesting to see that I might be capable of doing a whole host of other things I wouldn't have dreamed of. If you think your particular combination of skills, interests, and abilities adds up to only one particular kind of job or one specific career, these tests will open your eyes to the possibilities.

Test the Waters

If everyone's telling you that you have gifts in a particular area, but you're not entirely sure you see it, try taking those skills out for a test run. How? Get a part-time job or an internship that will draw on those skills.

For example, if you're good with animals, and people tell you that you're good with your hands, you may be leaning toward a career as a zookeeper. Call up a local zoo and ask if there are any openings for part-time employment.

The Worst Jobs in the World

Well...almost. The 2002 edition of the *Jobs Rated Almanac* by Les Krantz ranked 250 of the best and worst jobs. The bottom 5 jobs, based on work environment, are:

246. Taxi driver
247. NFL football player (although, there are some benefit$)
248. Race car driver
249. Firefighter
250. President of the United States of America

Nobody wants to hold *two* of the worst jobs in one lifetime. Which is why you never see retired NFL football players running for president of the United States.

(They'll probably *love* to have you come over to hose down the monkey habitat!)

If not, consider "auditing" a career, just like you'd audit a class. In other words, you're there, on the job, but you're just observing. It won't be as good as hands-on experience—and since you'll be unpaid, you probably won't be able to do this for more than a day or so—but it will give you a much closer look at a job than you'd get from a book or in a classroom. You might be surprised by how many professionals would be willing to let you shadow them.

Finally, look for volunteer opportunities. Many organizations would be happy to have your assistance, even as you're exploring possible career options. It isn't that you're necessarily looking for volunteer work that you'll eventually want to do for pay. But you may be able to snag volunteer assignments that exercise skills *similar* to those you'd be called upon to use in a traditional work environment.

Take Charge

I want to end this section with a strong, personal reminder: You are doing the work of assessing your skills—learning about yourself and your interests—so that you can take charge of your career and your life. It isn't busy work to help you *feel* like you're doing something productive. It also isn't a formula for cookie-cutter career suggestions.

Pinpointing your skills, interests, and abilities is vital to doing work that you will love for the rest of your life. Never forget that *your* career, *your* success, and *your* happiness are at stake here. You may feel inexperienced. You may lack confidence. You may be tempted to assume that everyone else knows best—and lean too heavily on what parents, counselors, friends, and relatives are telling you about your career prospects and what you should be doing with your life. Don't. Take charge of your life.

Recently, a high-school graduate of the class of 2002 told me he wants to be a residential architect, but he wasn't sure he was making the right choices for his career. We had the chance to talk a little about his future one afternoon.

"Have you ever talked to any architects who are doing what you want to do?" I asked. "You know—to find out where they went to school, what it's really like to do what they do for a living, or what they'd suggest you do to get into residential architecture?"

"Uh…no."

"Ever looked into what colleges around the country are really well known for their residential architecture programs?"

He paused. "Well, I asked the guidance counselor at school, and she didn't really know of any."

And so this young man, who apparently is talented and full of potential, is planning to go to a local junior college for a couple of years, get the basics out of the way, and then either get a job with an architecture firm or transfer to a nearby university, one that he *thinks* has a good architecture program.

To me, he seems to be "settling" for something. I could be wrong—it may be the absolutely best choice in the world for him. And perhaps I'm wrong to think that, at nineteen, he's 100 percent certain what he wants to do for a living. I'd probably recommend a serious residential-architecture track, and that might turn out to be totally wrong for him. He could get to college and figure out that the thing he loves most about residential architecture is the actual hands-on building of houses—not the designing, the estimating, the client meetings, or being stuck in an office all day. On the other hand, I'm baffled by the fact that, right now, he doesn't seem to be all that interested in taking the steps to succeed in the field he claims to be most passionate about.

This much is certain: No other living person will care as much about your life and your career as you do. If you begin to wonder if you're taking the easy way out or not really making the most of your skills and abilities, step back and ask yourself if you may be settling for second best. If the answer is yes or maybe, now is the time to change things. Now is the time to take charge of your life.

Chapter 4

In Search of the Burning Bush

I think I remember the conversation word for word.

I was in my second year of college, calling home from the pay phone in the ground-floor hallway of my dorm. My dad was on the other end, about four hundred miles away. "How am I supposed to know what God wants me to do with my life?" I asked, feeling torn between the career I thought I went to school for (youth minister) and the career that I felt drawn to more and more.

"What do you *want* to do?" Dad asked.

"I think I want to write. I definitely want to do something with writing."

"Then that's probably what God wants you to do."

He made it sound so simple: What do you *want* to do? What are you *good* at? Then go ahead and pursue that, and God will bless it. That was exactly the kind of advice I needed to hear.

SEARCHING FOR A SIGN

Every three years the parachurch ministry InterVarsity Christian Fellowship hosts a missions and evangelism conference at the University of Illinois in Urbana during the break between Christmas and New Year's Day. It's an inspiring event—attended by more than seventeen thousand students from all over the world and featuring internationally known Christian speakers. When

I worked for IVCF's publishing company, InterVarsity Press, a number of staff members were picked to work at "Urbana." Because I was a proofreader who knew most IVP books pretty well, I was always assigned to work in a book information booth in the cavernous exhibition hall.

The hall was ringed with hundreds of shelves packed with the books recommended by the Urbana speakers or written by them. My job was to answer people's questions about all of the titles available for sale and, using a computer printout, to point attendees to the specific shelf in the huge space where they could find the specific book they were searching for.

The most-requested books were on knowing God's will. That wasn't too shocking. The entire focus of the Urbana conference is on the spiritual needs of the world's various "people groups"—and how Christians can and should help meet those needs. The thousands of students who attend are at a critical point in their lives, trying to decipher what role they might play in world evangelism. So it's only natural for them to wonder, "Gee, what does God want me to do?" and "How can I know for certain that I'm following God's will?"

"Please Don't Send Me to Haiti!"

I don't know why it is. For some reason, Christians tend to suspect that the question, "What does God me to do?" will almost always lead to one answer: "God wants me to do exactly what I don't want to do."

This way of thinking reminds me of Marilyn Monroe. (No, not *that* Marilyn Monroe.) Marilyn was a young missionary—she couldn't have been older than twenty-five—who visited my church to talk about her work in Haiti and show slides of some of the people she had met, places she'd seen. During her presentation, she mentioned that two years earlier, when she had first started thinking seriously about missions, Haiti had been the country she dreaded the most.

"I remember running into my room, falling on the bed, and just crying, 'God, please don't send me to Haiti!'" she said. All of us in the congregation laughed at the joke: By saying that to God, of course, she virtually *guaranteed* she'd be going to Haiti. That's how it works. Just tell God you don't want to go somewhere, and you might as well start getting your shots and packing your bags. Tell God that you'd love to study law, grow Christmas trees, or work in a TV newsroom, and before you know it, he'll have you running an inner-city soup kitchen. Because God loves to send us where we don't want to go, to do things we don't want to do. This is how he builds our Christian character.

Well…not exactly.

According to *USA Today*, 6.2 million businesses in the United States are owned by women.

This concept of God is like all of those stupid computer hoaxes that keep popping up in our e-mail in-boxes: It taps into our worst fears, but in the end it's just an empty time-waster. It's a falsehood that distracts us from the real work we should be doing. God doesn't bless us with talents and interests just so he can see how much "character" we'll build by completely ignoring them. He isn't a mean-spirited, sly god who presses his ear to the wall trying to hear our hushed comments about what we'd most hate to do and then works to bring those very things to pass.

God loves you. He gave you skills and talents and interests so that you can glorify him through them and become the best person you can be.

God's Guarantee

So how does Marilyn Monroe's fear of going to Haiti fit into this picture? Within a couple of years of visiting our church, she decided to leave missionary work and return to the States.

I don't want to read too much into her story. But honestly, I've got to wonder if going to Haiti was really God's direction for her in the first place. Maybe it was. It could be that she was needed there for a specific length of time or that God really did want her to experience something important there, and then move on.

But maybe Marilyn ended up in Haiti because she saw the country's incredible poverty and spiritual needs and concluded that, being a Christian, she should offer to help. Or maybe a trusted spiritual advisor—pastor, counselor, friend—told her that she should go. It's even possible that some entirely well-meaning minister or missionary "guilted" her into going because of Haiti's needs and Marilyn's availability. So she went. Yet, based on everything I've heard about her since, it doesn't sound as if she was ever a good fit for Haiti or for missionary work in general. She didn't have the skills to do what was needed, and she didn't have a personal passion for that part of the world. Marilyn would have been a much happier person serving God in some other way, somewhere else.

See, that's God's guarantee when it comes to doing his will: He is able to use you wherever you end up. Granted, you might take a wrong turn here and there over the course of a lifetime. You may end up in a job "just because": because you are desperate, because you have unexpected financial needs, because you want to help a friend. No matter how you got here—and no matter where "here" is—God is ready, willing, and able to use you for his glory.

So relax. If you are truly trying to follow God, and if you heed the call of the interests, abilities, skills, and passions God has blessed you with, I believe you will be doing God's will.

What About Moses?

I realize that, no matter what, some people are still spazzing over the question of how your passions and skills can possibly lead you to doing something good for God. It's not enough to *believe* you're doing God's will in your career. You want to *know*.

Lightning. Earthquake. Heavenly trumpets. Free pizza for life. You want a *sign*.

Maybe even a sign like Moses had: A talking, burning bush that tells you exactly what you're supposed to do and how you're supposed to do it.

In case you were out getting popcorn when the movie started, let's recap the Moses story.

Moses was born in Egypt to Hebrew parents after Pharaoh decreed that all male Hebrew babies were to be thrown into the river and killed. (Egypt's leadership was afraid of being outnumbered and overthrown by their Hebrew slaves.) So Moses' mom saved him by hiding him immediately after he was born. Three months later she "threw him into the river" (ironic, don'tcha think?) in a little waterproof basket that took him downstream to Pharaoh's very own household, where he was rescued.

Fast-forward to Moses as an adult.

What good is it for a man to gain the whole world, and yet lose or forfeit his very self?

—JESUS CHRIST

Although he was raised in privilege in Pharaoh's home, Moses never forgot he was born a Hebrew. So when he came across an Egyptian who was abusing a Hebrew slave, Moses killed the Egyptian and buried the body in the sand. It didn't take Sherlock Holmes to solve the crime—and soon Moses was the object of a Pharaoh-led manhunt.

He ended up hiding out in Midian, where he married, had a son, and began working for his father-in-law as a shepherd. And it was when he was tending his father-in-law's flocks that he came across a bush lit with fire. Since the bush wasn't getting burned up as a result, Moses got curious. And that's when he heard the voice of God, with a message that was going to change both Moses' life and the course of history for the Hebrew people.

The thing is, I think, Moses got his burning bush because he was headed in the wrong direction. He didn't survive Pharaoh's killing hand at birth so he could become a shepherd. Not even a really good shepherd. He also wasn't meant to thwart Egyptian oppression by killing one abusive man. God intended something much different for Moses: a role as the freedom leader for thousands upon thousands of Hebrew families. But Moses would never have moved into that new career on his own; God needed something dramatic to grab his attention and set him on the right track. Hence: the Burning Bush.

If you're actively working to follow God in your life, chances are God isn't going to need to grab you by the throat and give you a shake. You only need a visit from God if you're likely to miss the miracle he has in store for you. All the same, if you *do* see a bush that's burning without becoming charcoal, keep your eyes and ears open. Even if things have been going great. Because there's one other reason why God might come right out and tell you it's time to do something different: God may have something even better in store for you and your gifts. Something you can't even begin to imagine right now.

DRAMATIC LEAPS

Meet computer-repair technician Michael. Michael loves working with computers, and he loves helping people get the most use possible out of their machines. Unlike Christina, his coworker on the repair bench, he enjoys greeting customers when they walk through the door and talking with them about their computer problems. It helps him feel as if he's not just working on cold, lifeless circuit boards and wires. He's not just testing a glitchy network card or rescuing data from someone's crashed hard drive. He's helping someone's small business stay up and running. He's making sure some kid is able to turn in her homework on time. He's helping a housebound grandmother stay in touch with her grandkids over the Internet.

Christina loves harassing Michael about his fondness for customer contact. She'd be happy if customers left their computers outside in a box, rang the office doorbell, and quickly ran away without saying a word. "I mean, the whole reason I wanted to work with computers was because I liked being around technology more than people," Christina says. To her, Michael's "people-person" skills are a liability.

But she nevertheless has to admit that Michael's so-called liability hasn't had a negative impact on his work. In fact, Christina is the first to praise Michael's uncanny ability to diagnose obscure hardware conflicts, find just the right software patches on the Internet, and carry out nerve-racking repairs by hand when other techies would have simply ordered a new piece of equipment.

To be honest, Michael's combination of skills is worth a lot more than his boss is paying him. But Michael isn't too concerned about his hourly wage. He loves his work, he and Christina get along really well (despite her playful harassment), and he's content.

"At Eighteen I Took Off for Paris"

At age eighteen I got my heart broken and instead of sensibly going to university, I took off for Paris.

I stayed in a friend's apartment but only had $150 in the world and couldn't find a job anywhere. I was down to my last few francs when I wandered into an English bookshop and tearoom on the Rue de Rivoli and asked for work. Miraculously they hired me for sales. I had no career plan at all, but I loved books, my French improved from good to fluent, and I learned a lot about getting along with people from different cultural backgrounds. When they finally offered me a job as department manager, I realized that I didn't want to spend my life in retail. So I left and went home to England.

The language skills, my knowledge of Paris, and the confidence gained by "conquering" a foreign city proved invaluable over the years. Further down the road I landed one job purely because of my familiarity with Paris and the language.

—TANIA CASSELLE

Then one day a very well-dressed woman pulls up in a gleaming Jaguar. She's there to pick up her laptop, a top-of-the-line model that was having problems recognizing its installed memory chips.

Michael met her at the counter out front.

"I realize I'm about five hours earlier than you told me to come back, but I need that machine," she said, obviously nervous. "There's a multimedia presentation on that machine that I have to give in about two hours. Is there any way you can put a rush on it?"

"Actually, I think I've fixed the problem, but there are still two more tests I need to run."

She sighed.

"Tell you what," Michael said. "Why don't you step back into the repair room and watch me finish it up? Most people would just as soon not see the inside of their machine, but it might make the time go faster than just sitting out here and flipping through a two-year-old issue of *People*."

"Thanks," she said with a smile. "I'd like that. And it will give me a chance to see if you guys are really worth what you charge!"

Forty minutes later the laptop was fixed and ready for the customer's presentation. As the woman handed over her American Express, Michael noticed that it said the customer was a doctor. *And a pretty successful one,* Michael thought, *judging from the Jaguar and the money she invested in this machine.*

"You're a doctor?" he asked.

"I'm an oral surgeon." She paused. "You could be one too, you know. Or any other kind of surgeon, if you wanted to."

Michael swiped her credit card through the reader then stopped. "Me? I'm a computer tech."

"I know. But I watched you work. With your concentration and dexterity, I think you've got the makings of a good surgeon. And you seem comfortable with people too. In my business, that's called 'bedside manner.' And it's something they don't teach in any medical school."

"You're serious?"

The customer laughed. "I'm not offering you a job or anything, just throwing it out as something to think about."

"I'll do that," Michael said, suddenly grinning to himself. "Really."

When he told Christina what the customer had said, she couldn't stop laughing for a full minute.

If Michael's story sounds like pure fiction, let's change the wording a little bit. Basically, the customer was telling him that instead of being a fixer of computer problems, he could be a fixer of people problems. Is that such a big stretch from the call that Jesus gave to a couple of guys to move up from being fishers of fish to being fishers of people? I don't think so.

In the New Testament's gospel of Matthew, Jesus is walking beside the Sea of Galilee when he notices two men out in a boat, fishing. Simon Peter and his brother, Andrew, are doing what they've probably done every day of their working lives: sitting in a boat on the water, throwing their nets over the side, and hauling in their catch. Just another workday.

Everyone else on shore who shielded their eyes and looked out to sea saw a fishing boat with two men working in it. Jesus looked out and saw something more. Maybe he thought about the patience fishermen need when the fish aren't swimming their way and the nets keep coming up empty. Maybe he thought about the courage fishermen need when the wind kicks up, the waves get choppy, and storms come sweeping in. Maybe he thought about the teamwork required for fishermen to haul in a net bulging with the day's catch. And maybe he recognized that the fishing skills Simon Peter and Andrew had developed on the water could be put to a much wider purpose on dry land.

Whatever things Jesus knew about the men's past and present, he invited them to experience a bigger future: "Come, follow me," he said, "and I will make you fishers of men" (Matthew 4:19). Amazingly they did just that. And the whole scenario repeated itself when Jesus walked on and met two other fishing brothers, James and John. Immediately, "they left the boat and their father and followed him" (verse 22).

Now, if this robed stranger hadn't happened to walk across the beach that day, it's doubtful that Simon Peter, Andrew, James, and John would have decided to stop fishing for fish and start fishing for souls. It would have been just another day at the beach. And that would have been fine. But instead, Jesus came along and told them they were capable of doing something bigger and better. Some small voice inside them must have told them he was right, because they immediately dropped what they were doing and set out on a new career.

About 6 percent of all workers have more than one job.

This visit from God wasn't corrective. As far as we know, these first disciples weren't heading down the wrong path or running away from God before they were called to follow Jesus. They were good men going about their daily lives. Rather, God broke through the ordinariness of the day to let them know he had a new mission in store for them. It would build on their past skills, but it would also lead them to become quite different men.

I think God still speaks to us today when he wants us to make a dramatic leap upward and onward. He may not use a burning bush at all. In fact, he might speak to you through a passing stranger who apparently recognizes abilities and potential yet to be explored. But I believe you'll know when it's God who is doing the speaking. You'll know in your heart and your soul that it's an invitation to drop what you're doing, follow him, and grow.

WILL AND GRACE

If you're wondering whether a particular choice is meshing with God's will— and you're not getting a strong leading one way or the other—it can help to work through the following questions and see just where you stand.

Does it fit with Scripture? When in doubt, remember that God has already

revealed his will for humanity in the Bible. He is not going to ask us to do anything that departs from the truth he has already given. We won't glorify him
if we choose to do something contrary to Scripture.

Will there be gray areas? Quite possibly. They might even change shades
from person to person. One science teacher won't have any problem with a
class discussion about evolution; another might feel that to give evolution any
credibility at all would mean sacrificing his Christian beliefs. One hospice
worker will be able to comfort those in the final stages of an AIDS-related
death; another hospice worker might find it difficult to get beyond her own
feelings about the lifestyles that sometimes lead to HIV infection. You'll get
help for working through any gray areas by taking an honest look at your own
beliefs and temperament and by considering the other questions listed here.

Does it feel *right in your heart?* The heart loves to play tricks on us—hey,
we've probably all got some embarrassing dating stories we'd like to keep
buried forever—but it can also help us to discern the right path. (Think "conscience.") Are you considering a job you'd rather not list on a résumé? A job
that involves doing something you wouldn't want to admit to the government,
your pastor, your mother? Something you wouldn't like seeing advertised on a
billboard above the busiest street in your community?

Do you want to do it? In a nutshell: Are you going to be happy doing this
job? Is it going to meet some of your personal needs—financial, creative, or
experiential (that is, giving you something you can carry with you and build
on in future jobs/careers)? If you're considering a job requiring a move, it's
definitely worth asking how well you'll be able to settle into a new community. Whether you'll adjust to leaving family or friends behind. Whether you'll
really be able to cope with subzero winters, earthquakes, a new big city or
small town, or constant sunshine and the annoying sound of the surf going in
and out.

What do your trusted friends and advisors say about it? I'm not suggesting
that you let someone else make the decision for you, tempting as that might

be. But it can often help to get input and feedback from people whose counsel you trust and who don't have a vested interest in the outcome.

Input and *feedback* might seem like synonyms, but I see them as two different steps. To me, *input* means laying out the facts or the choices and simply
asking your friend or advisor: "What do you think?" or "What would you do
if you were in my shoes? Why?" *Feedback* is the next step, where you go
beyond the straight facts to share your own thoughts about the situation and
ask for their assessment of your thought processes, asking questions like,
"What part of the puzzle am I missing here?" or "Am I making this into a bigger deal than it really is? Is the solution staring right at me?"

If at first you don't succeed, you're about average.

—Anonymous

Do the pieces seem to be falling into place in a clear-cut way? The phrase
"when one door closes, another one opens" can't be found anywhere in the
Bible. But often, God does use our circumstances to lead us in one direction
or another. If you find yourself at a decision-making crossroads, try stepping
back and recalling exactly how you got there. It can be a lot easier to see God's
hand at work in your life by looking at the past rather than the future. If it
seems you've found open doors along a certain path, it might be wise to continue on that path and see where it takes you.

Have you prayed about it? Prayer gets two things done at once: It makes it
possible for us to grow as believers who are sincerely trying to follow God's
leading, and it softens our hearts to the point where we are ready to hear whatever God might want to tell us. In other words, it tells God, "Here I am, ready
to follow wherever you want to lead me." And to pray that prayer honestly

requires that we give up any certainty we might have about what's best for us and let God correct or encourage us.

And if you're still baffled about what God's will might be? Well, that's where grace comes in.

In some corporations, the unspoken motto is, "It's easier to ask forgiveness than permission." That is, the real go-getters in the company weigh all the variables, gather their courage, and make the decisions that they feel will be best for the company. They bravely go forward in good faith, believing that they're doing the right thing. They take a risk. Sometimes they succeed brilliantly. Sometimes they crash and burn just as brilliantly. And when that happens, they take the heat. But if they never took that first step, they'd *never* succeed. And they wouldn't learn any of the valuable lessons that come with failure.

Even though we are making decisions out of a sincere desire to follow God's will, we might still fail. Or we might be distracted by something—an incredible salary, a romantic relationship, prestige—that temporarily draws us away from God's will.

Regardless of the cause, if we misstep along the way to God's best for us, he is ready and willing to forgive us. He won't reprimand us, fine us, or put us on two months' probation. He'll wash away the mistake, help us to make the best of a bad situation, and give us the courage we need to move on and serve him to the best of our abilities.

Chapter 5

Dare to Dream

"What do you want to be when you grow up?"

When we're young, that's a pretty common question, with some equally common answers: doctor, lawyer, teacher, police officer, firefighter, astronaut. If we come from a long line of farmers or politicians, we might mention a job associated with agriculture or politics. If our parents are enthusiastic cooks, we might want to be a chef. When we're young, we associate most strongly with the professions we see the most—either on TV or in our families.

But there are lots of career opportunities out there that go far, far beyond the occupations typically portrayed on TV ("vampire slayer" and "sex columnist" aside). Consider, for example:

- beekeeper
- bounty hunter
- film editor
- forest fire lookout
- funeral home cosmetologist
- graphic designer
- hot-air balloon pilot
- performance artist
- photographer
- product name developer
- restaurant critic

- romance novelist
- taxidermist
- travel writer
- voice-over actor
- yoga instructor

Brady White has been playing Santa Claus for more than twenty years—and earns more than sixty dollars a minute donning the red suit for big-name Hollywood clients and upscale stores such as Cartier, Neiman-Marcus, and Saks Fifth Avenue.

Chuck Street flies high over the streets of Los Angeles in his own helicopter as a traffic reporter for local media.

Paige Novick took five thousand dollars and an idea and turned them into a multimillion-dollar accessories company that develops handbags, makeup cases, and clothing.

Leslie Strahl is an animal ambulance driver, rescuing cats in trees, helping birds with broken wings, and once even pulling a cow out of a ditch.

By day, Teresa Rollins is a tour guide at the Country Music Hall of Fame in Nashville; by night, she works as an impersonator of country-music legend Patsy Cline.

Rob Klepper travels all over the United States in his job with a public-relations agency that introduces travel writers and photographers to interesting people and places.

Jeanneane Palczewski is a self-employed Kindermusik instructor, using music, movement, and play to enhance the development of children from infancy to seven years of age.

The list is endless. (Or at least it would need a much longer book.) But the point is not that there are lots of people doing lots of interesting and unusual things in the world. The point is that you can be one of them. For nearly everyone reading this book, the career opportunities you can take hold of are limited only by your imagination.

That isn't to say you should turn your back on your childhood dream of becoming a police officer or doctor and shoot for something more exotic. It's just that sometimes we can only see the possibilities that are directly in front of us. So we limit ourselves to those choices, like a camera that's stuck on "zoom." To really see the possibilities, you have to get out of zoom mode and step back for an IMAX-like view. Maybe you'll weigh all of the choices and just be that much more certain that being a police officer or a doctor is exactly what you're supposed to be doing right now. Or maybe you'll suddenly realize that your talents, interests, and skills could actually work in an entirely different kind of job—one you didn't even know existed.

If a man does only what is required of him, he is a slave. If a man does more than is required of him, he is a free man.

—CHINESE PROVERB

While you're giving some thought to some interesting "whats," don't overlook the interesting "wheres." Sure, you can move back to your hometown after college, get a job doing something that you love, become active in the church you grew up in (or swore you'd never be caught dead in), marry your high-school sweetheart, watch your kids graduate from your old high school, and when it's all said and done, get buried in the cemetery where you used to swipe plastic flowers as a kid.

There's nothing wrong with that.

But there's a big world out there. And if you're open to dreaming and planning "outside the box" when it comes to careers, maybe you should give equal time to thinking about where in the world you want to go with your life. Think about where you can be the most effective—as an employee or business owner and as a human being. Consider how a change of scenery might help make you a different person—for better or worse.

WHERE IN THE WORLD DO YOU BELONG?

Some jobs and careers pretty much dictate where you're going to live. If you want to work as a fashion photographer for *Vogue* magazine, you'll probably need to live in or near Manhattan. Disney animators might end up in Florida, California, or Paris. Ski instructors are going to need to live near snow—and big inclines.

Other jobs are more flexible in location but still require you to follow the work, at least to some extent. Not every community can provide enough patients for a new doctor in town; not every neighborhood needs a new restaurant. Church pastors in search of new positions have to either go where there is an opening or start a church of their own.

Finally, there are those jobs that can be done just about anywhere. Consulting is one. You don't have to live in a major metropolis in order to be a successful consultant for businesses across the country and around the world.

Okay. We've nailed down the logical approach in the three preceding paragraphs. Will the job require you to live someplace specific? Then that's where you'll live if you end up doing what you think you want to do. Is the location door wide open or partially cracked? Then you can weigh the economics involved in living in a new place, the cost of moving versus staying where you are now, the emotional impact of moving away from or closer to friends, relatives, significant others, and on and on and on—checking off all of the neat little boxes on your logical list and guaranteeing that you'll make the wisest, most practical decision.

But what about the not-so-cut-and-dried considerations? To round out your decision-making process, ask yourself two more questions:

- Where do you think God can use you best?
- Where do you think there is the greatest need for your abilities?

If the scales are pretty evenly balanced between different opportunities, the answers you come up with to these questions can help tip you in one direction while continuing to keep you focused on doing what God has equipped you to do in the world.

Taking a good look at a couple other questions may help you in your decision-making process as well.

Who in the World Do You Want to Be?

Any job you take will offer opportunities and challenges. Some will be positive, helping you learn more about yourself and the world. Others will be negative, testing your patience, your pocketbook, maybe even your faith. Not every fun experience will be beneficial for you as a human being. And not every "bad" experience should be avoided; we can learn a lot from life's rough times.

But where you choose to live, work, and have a personal impact on the world can actually help to shape who you become as a human being. For example, you might feel that you could honestly have your best witness—and do something you love doing—by playing piano in a bar. (Hey, that's how Elton John and Billy Joel got started.) But if drinking alcohol is a problem for you, making your living in a bar would not be your wisest move. It's an unnecessary temptation. And working under such conditions is likely to turn you into someone you don't want to be.

A 2001 Maritz Poll showed that Americans most respect the careers of teacher (No. 1), doctor (No. 2), and social worker (No. 3). The least-respected profession? Politician.

Or let's say that you're passionate about nursing, and you've just received a fantastic job offer from a health clinic in the city of your dreams. But let's also say that the clinic is one of the few places in the city where women with low incomes can get abortions—and you don't believe that abortion is a good moral choice. You might be tempted to take the job simply because it's a good offer, you need the money, and you think that you can overlook this one aspect of the clinic. Or maybe you believe you could change the clinic's way of doing business once you're working "on the inside." Don't kid yourself. The salary might be appealing, and there might be a lot of job duties that you'd sincerely love doing. But if you believe that abortion is wrong, and you are required to assist in performing abortions, you will be torn apart inside. You will end up hating either your employer or yourself. And neither result is worth a paycheck.

Where Does Family Fit?

For many of us, who we are and how grounded we feel in any one place depends a lot on how geographically close we are to our families. There's no right answer here—at least not one that any book can offer you. I know people who have moved three thousand miles and one ocean away from their families. I know others whose parents and siblings have never lived more than ten minutes apart.

If you do feel pulled to a distant destination, you can take comfort from the fact that thanks to e-mail, instant messaging, cellular phones, voice mail, and air and train transportation, it has never been easier to stay in touch with those we care about. Can those things take the place of a hug when you need one? or a friendly face when you feel surrounded by strangers? or counsel from someone who knows you better than you even know yourself? No. But they can help keep you connected, informed, and encouraged.

I'll share a personal bias here: If circumstances permit it, I think it's better to move away and experience life on your own, at least for a while. It takes you out of your comfort zone, forces you to reach out and make new friends, and teaches you valuable things about yourself and the world around you. For some, going away to college is enough; after four years, they've discovered that they really do want to remain close to their family. But others move away and discover an inner strength that they may not have found closer to home. They realize that they can strike out successfully on their own with the support of their loved ones and forge new and exciting lives.

Whether you go, how far you go, and how long you stay there are between you and your family. Ultimately, though, the choice is yours.

It's a Small, Small World

Someone told me recently that he was impressed with how many well-known and influential men and women have come out of small towns. (Having

---

"I Never Really Had a Career Plan"

My first job postcollege was working for the Population Reference Bureau, Inc., a nonprofit clearinghouse for demographic information, located in Washington, D.C. I'd majored in international relations in college, with a specialty in Third World development, and I was passionate about population issues. I'd done an internship at PRB the summer between my junior and senior years, and they hired me in the fall after I graduated.

I was sort of a Jill-of-all-trades for a little while—doing research, some editorial work, and some computer stuff. After a couple of months, I found a niche for myself as the associate editor of their monthly newsletter/magazine hybrid called *Population Today*. After doing that for a couple of years, I switched over (in-house) to working on an international project, coordinating production of publications for developing-country policy makers, which led to one trip around the world and another trip to Kenya. I quit after five years there to move to St. Louis.

I never really had a career plan. I just wanted to do work that I enjoyed with people who I enjoyed working with. I also wanted to do something that helped others.

—JANINE ADAMS

grown up in a small town myself, my first reaction was, "Well, yeah. They're hypermotivated to get out!") If you grew up in a small town, maybe you've thought that your career options are naturally going to be more limited than those of the people who live in the nearest major metropolis: "Big city" equals "big opportunities." Or maybe you see limited career opportunities because you don't know anyone who is doing what you'd like to do: "No connections" means "no luck."

First, some good news. Yes, we're all living on a very big planet. But when it comes to connecting with other people—people who can help you throughout your career—it's a small, small world after all. Big city or tiny town, well known or not—it doesn't matter. Opportunities for expanding your career choices and developing important relationships are available to everyone.

Who Do You Know?

There's this belief out there that career success has a lot to do with "who you know." Here's the truth: That's absolutely right.

Shocked? Don't be.

If you were a manager looking for a new employee, who would you rather hire: an experienced stranger or an experienced friend? If you were a self-employed businesswoman shopping around for a new accountant, who would you rather talk taxes with: a guy you found while leafing through the Yellow Pages or a guy who was recommended by a mutual acquaintance? Or imagine that you're driving back to work after lunch, and your car suddenly starts shuddering and backfiring. When it comes to a dead stop, with smoke pouring out from under the hood, who would you rather turn to for roadside assistance: the mechanic who fixed your best friend's car last week or the one who runs the most ads on the radio?

Face it: We all prefer to deal with people we know or people who come to us through people we trust. It's human nature. It isn't part of some dark plot to keep out talented people who don't have the "right" connections. People simply like working with their friends.

Sound like bad news for you? It's not. Feel as if you don't have enough friends or the right connections? You do. Really.

Maybe you've heard of the game Six Degrees of Kevin Bacon. Three college guys named Mike Ginelli, Craig Fass, and Brian Turtle invented it. The goal of the game is to connect actor Kevin Bacon with any other Hollywood actor through the films or television shows they've done together, using a maximum of six steps.

If you're stumped already, you can let a computer play the game for you. For example, I just ran the name "Marisa Tomei" through the "Oracle of Bacon" at the University of Virginia computer center at www.cs.virginia.edu/oracle. (How do college kids *think* of these things?) Marisa has a "Bacon number" of two. She starred in *The Paper* with an actress named Lynn Thigpen. (Yeah, me neither.) And Lynn Thigpen appeared in a 2001 movie called *Novocaine* with—*ta da!*—Kevin Bacon.

The greatest pleasure I know is to do a good action by stealth, and have it found out by accident.

—CHARLES LAMB

I tried fooling the Oracle by picking a name from moviedom's way-distant past: silent film comedian Buster Keaton. Buster was huge in the 1920s, but he was pretty much retired by the mid-1940s. I figured that the chance of finding a Kevin Bacon connection was slim. Silly me. Apparently, clips from Keaton's movies were used in the 1990 film *Buster's Bedroom,* which also featured Donald Sutherland. Sutherland went on to appear in the 1991 film *JFK* with Kevin Bacon. Again, just two films removed.

I could easily spend a couple of senseless hours plugging name after name into the Kevin Bacon database (okay, I actually *did* spend a couple of hours doing that), but that's not the point. The point is that while Six Degrees of Kevin Bacon may be a fun trivia game for true movie addicts, it highlights an amazing fact about the intrinsic power of our real-world relationships. And that's how we get to the subject of networking.

Researchers call it the "small-world" effect. It's also known as "six degrees of separation." (Which, if you want my semieducated guess, is how those three college guys came up with Six Degrees of Kevin Bacon; any actor's name would have worked, but "Kevin Bacon" kinda rhymes with "separation." "Six Degrees of Cameron Diaz" just wouldn't fly.)

In a nutshell, the idea of "six degrees of separation" came out of the work of psychologist Stanley Milgram, about thirty to forty years ago. Milgram stumbled upon the startling fact that, apparently, everyone in America can be connected to everyone else by a chain of only five or six intermediaries. How is that possible?

According to British physicist Robert Matthews, sociologists figure that each of us typically has around three hundred friends and acquaintances, people we know on a first-name basis. Well, if each of those three hundred friends has three hundred friends, that means we're only two people away from connecting with ninety thousand people...and three away from twenty-seven million. And, maybe most bizarre of all, these relationships cross ethnic, cultural, religious, and economic boundaries.

So, yes, career success depends a lot on who you know. Dropping the name of a mutual friend can help you get your foot in the door for an interview, an internship, maybe even a job. But if you're thinking you don't know anyone who can possibly help you learn something about auditioning for off-Broadway theater, becoming a certified public accountant, designing houses, creating video games, or working at a publishing house, I'm willing to bet that you're wrong. Make your needs and interests known, and you'll end up connecting with many more helpful, influential people than you thought possible.

Expanding Your Universe

To some people, *networking* is a bad word. They think it means being a false friend in order to work the angles in your favor. Being manipulative. Using people for your benefit.

That's not networking. To me, networking simply means the sharing of career or work information between friends or colleagues. It's a mutual, two-way dialogue that enhances our personal relationships. It's not squeezing the other person for insider information, then dropping the relationship the minute you get what you need.

Everybody can take advantage of the power of networking. But it does require one huge step: You've got to ask for help.

You might be best friends with major movers and shakers in your field. But if you never let anyone know what advice you're looking for or what career help you need, you're not much better off than the hermit who can't remember when he last saw another human being. As weird as it might sound, people will want to help you. But you've got to take the first step and let them know exactly what you're looking for. If you want to know whether anyone knows someone in the automotive industry, ask—and tell your friends and acquaintances why you're asking: "I'd like to learn more about designing cars for General Motors," or "I'd love to get a job with Toyota." The more specific you are, the more your contacts will be able to help you. Plus, if they know exactly why you're seeking their help, they might come up with some alternative solutions you haven't thought of.

Finding folks to network with isn't hard. Consider the following groups:

- *Friends and relatives.* Start with the people you know best. Tell them what you're interested in and the kind of contacts you're looking for. Then check in with them in a week or two; if you just sit back and wait for them to get back to you, you might be waiting a long time. Let them know this request is important to you. Just try not to nag them so much that they get a restraining order.

- *Classmates*. If you're in school now—whether high school or college—ask classmates about their connections. You might be surprised to learn that someone you've known since kindergarten has family ties to someone who can help you realize your dream career.

  If you're in high school, and you're wondering whether to go to a local junior college or a four-year school, I'd encourage you to consider the four-year school—assuming your career could benefit from it—simply because you'll meet a much wider variety of people from a much wider variety of places. In short, your networking reach will be far greater than that of someone whose connections stop at the next county.

- *Special-interest groups*. What's *your* special-interest? No matter what it is, I can almost guarantee you that there's a trade association devoted to it. Don't believe me? Hike down to the reference shelves of your public library and flip through the multivolume *Encyclopedia of Associations*. There you'll find names, addresses, and other information about thousands of special-interest groups that can help you in your search for the perfect career. If you're not yet working in a particular association's field, it won't hurt to call them up and ask about membership rates for students and other interested individuals.

You can also log on to the Web and search for associations related to your area of interest. For example, if you're interested in teaching therapeutic riding —that is, working with horses to help handicapped or disabled individuals— go to your favorite search engine (mine is currently Google at www.google. com) and search for: *"therapeutic riding" associations*.

But don't stop with just finding out about an association. Many offer helpful publications in addition to their newsletters and magazines. Many also post job openings and information about upcoming seminars on their Web sites. Read the information, attend a seminar (if possible), meet the people in the organization, and get involved.

Also, don't overlook online forums related to your special interest. The

Internet and the Web have created incredible opportunities for networking. Almost every day I get job leads and career encouragement from dozens of other freelance writers whom I've never met face to face. Some live several hours away; some live on other continents. But I wouldn't have communicated with any of them if I hadn't first made contact in online forums devoted to professional freelance writing.

No "Buts" Allowed

One of the biggest hurdles between you and your dream job isn't geography or a lack of networking opportunities. It's you. Or rather, your inner censor, the voice inside that loves nothing better than explaining in painful detail why something won't work or why you can't do it.

This is the voice that, when you hear about a dream job you'd like to pursue, starts "but"-ing in:

"Well, you'd be great at that, of course, but…"

"You tried that once, but…"

"Sure, you were able to make it through the interview, but…"

The Pilot Pen Corporation of America has uncovered some—well, let's just call them "intriguing"—facts about "pen psychology" in the workplace.

- Workers who use red pens (and men who use pencils) are most likely to think the boss is nice.
- Men who use expensive pens, green pens, and purple pens feel the most secure in their jobs. (But, then, I'd think you'd have to feel pretty secure to use a purple pen at work…)
- Women who use green pens, purple pens, and who hardly ever use a pen at all are most likely to be bored at work.

With just one little three-letter word, our internal censor is able to acknowledge our great ideas and good dreams and then rip the rug out from under our feet, pointing out all of the reasons why we will never succeed.

"I would love to be a psychologist, *but* I'd have to go back to school."

"I would love to finish that novel, *but* I can't really find the time to sit down and write."

"I've got a terrific idea for a new business, *but* it would be a real gamble to quit my job."

I'm not suggesting that we set aside reality or ignore logical arguments. But I *am* suggesting that most of us would go a lot further toward realizing our deepest desires if we made the conscious choice to shut up our inner censors.

In his book *Do It! Let's Get Off Our Buts,* Peter McWilliams makes some powerful points:

We are all, right now, living the life we choose.

This choice, of course, is not a single, monumental choice. No one decides, for example, "I'm going to move to L.A., and in five years I will be a waiter in a so-so restaurant, planning to get my 8-x-10's done real soon so that I can find an agent and become a star," or "I'm going to marry a dreadful person and we'll live together in a loveless marriage, staying together only for the kids, who I don't much like, either."

No. The choices I'm talking about here are made daily, hourly, moment by moment.

Do we try something new, or stick to the tried-and-true? Do we take a risk, or eat what's already on our dish? Do we ponder a thrilling adventure, or contemplate what's on TV? Do we walk over and meet that interesting stranger, or do we play it safe? Do we indulge our heart, or cater to our fear?

The bottom-line question: Do we pursue what we want, or do we do what's comfortable?

For the most part, most people most often choose comfort—the familiar, the time-honored, the well-worn but well-known. After a life-time of choosing between comfort and risk, we are left with the life we currently have.

And it was all of our own choosing.[1]

Not to sound like the old grandfather sitting on the porch swing and passing along wisdom to the young'uns, but...

My prayer is that you will never find yourself stuck in a life you do not love. That you will never—at any point in your career—stop, drop your head, and ask yourself, "How in the world did I ever end up *here?*" That you will never settle for a job that pays the bills but doesn't meet your deeper needs.

But you know what? It just might happen. For all kinds of really good and sensible reasons, you might well find yourself feeling stuck or at a dead end, frustrated with your career and maybe even with your life.

If that ever happens in your life, I also have another prayer: that you will never, ever stop dreaming. Because God does not want us to languish in unproductive, unfulfilling lives. He wants to use us in ways that bring glory to his name and joy to our souls. As long as we have a dream of something better, we can take steps—maybe small baby steps and maybe giant leaps—to reach our goals and turn our dreams into realities.

Part 2

Finding Your Path in the Workplace

Chapter 6

Putting Your Passion to Work

When I drove into Downers Grove, Illinois, my car was already jerking its way up inclines, throwing off signs—which I chose to ignore—that I was going to need a new transmission sooner rather than later. At that point, I wasn't in a position to do anything about it. So I pressed the gas pedal to the floor and chugged my way up every hill. I kept one foot on the brake and one on the gas at every stop sign, just to keep the motor running in my aging boat of a car. I didn't have a choice.

I had to get to my job interview at InterVarsity Press, a Christian book and magazine publisher I'd barely heard of but where I absolutely *had* to get a job. IVP was the last publisher on my list. If they said no, I didn't know what was next. The mall? McDonald's? My parents' house?

I was desperate. For two months I'd been living with a couple of college friends in a house that was either half-renovated or half-crumbling (depending on your point of view), trying with increasing anxiety to get my foot in the door at a Chicago-area Christian publishing house. I had a bachelor's degree…and not much else to offer. Not too surprisingly, I wasn't exactly winning over the human-resources folks who were interviewing me.

When I began my job search, my real goal was to start in the editorial department as either a proofreader or an editorial assistant, then slowly work my way up to being a full-fledged book editor. I couldn't imagine anything I'd love more than being a book editor. But entry-level editorial positions proved hard to come by. And like I said, I was getting desperate. So here I was, going to an interview at the last company on my list, for a job in the—gulp—mailroom. And I got it.

My foot was in the door. Over the next six or seven years, I'd pry that door open little by little, working my way up to full-time proofreader, then marketing copywriter, changing companies after five years, changing again after another year, then eventually becoming a dual PR person/assistant editor. Two years later, I finally reached my goal of being a *real* editor.

I offer all of this as a way of contrasting my own stumbling experiences with those of my friend Michael Maudlin.

Mickey was hired as a full-time proofreader at IVP a month or so before I got there. (Yep. Stole the job right out from under me.) Within a year he was a book editor. In fact, it was his promotion that allowed me to leave the mailroom and take his spot in the editorial department. Over the next dozen or so years, Mickey grew as a book editor, earning the respect of his colleagues and settling into a position that he probably could have retired in, if he had wanted to. But Mickey told me he was beginning to miss the challenges that had made his earlier progress so interesting. So he left IVP to become an editor at *Christianity Today* magazine. Today he is the top editor at CT's *Marriage Partnership* magazine.

I used to have bouts of jealousy when it came to comparing my own career growth with Mickey's. While I got sidetracked into other departments and rejected opportunities that might have guaranteed similar editorial longevity—for example, choosing not to go to graduate school in theology, which would have helped me at the academically oriented IVP—Mickey seemed to shoot straight up the career ladder, moving steadily from success to success.

But I'm not jealous anymore.

Here's why: As much as I told myself I wanted to be a full-time book editor, my heart really wasn't in it. Not ever. Since I was about ten years old, I haven't *really* wanted to be anything but a freelance writer. But that seemed so impossible/tenuous/unrealistic that I ended up picking a similar, word-focused job that would provide a greater measure of financial stability. So I searched for jobs that were close to freelance writing but also provided a steady paycheck, paid vacation days, and health coverage. And I tried to feed my freelancing needs by writing short stories in my spare time. As a result, I didn't go out of my way to navigate the book editor career ladder. I had a rougher time of it, as a result.

If a man hasn't discovered something that he will die for, he isn't fit to live.

—MARTIN LUTHER KING JR.

I don't know that Mickey Maudlin had any special vision for where he wanted to be five, ten, or twenty years down the road in his career. What he did have, though—and continues to have, from all of the signs of his success—is a real passion for being an editor. From the moment he stepped into that proofreading job at InterVarsity Press, he put that passion to work. And he reaped the rewards.

ALL THE WORLD'S A STAGE

As Mr. Shakespeare once suggested, if all the world's a stage, that makes all of us actors on it. Think about that in terms of your passions, your career goals, your job. Whether you're just starting out in your first full-time job or you're wondering if maybe you should rethink your career and try something different, you benefit by seeing yourself as an actor first.

"But don't most actors have to make ends meet by waiting tables?" you might ask. Well, I'm not talking about *literally* being an actor (unless that's what you're passionate about). I'm talking about the benefits of playing a role in your work life, whether you're an office clerk, construction worker, truck driver, teacher, candy maker, broccoli farmer, minister, postal carrier, insurance underwriter, tour guide, or anything else.

One of my favorite mottos for beginning writers who are struggling to reach the next level—maybe they're wanting to move up from writing for *Dairy Goat Daily* to *Reader's Digest*—is this: *Act like the writer you want to be.* That advice isn't exclusively for writers, of course. Wanna be a Washington lobbyist? Act like the lobbyist you want to be. Wanna be a funeral director? Act like the funeral director you want to be. Get the idea?

Let's break down what it means to "act like the _____ you want to be." It doesn't involve lying or anything like that. It doesn't involve a fake ID. It involves nurturing a "mind-set of success." In other words, if we start *acting* like the successful people we want to be, we'll eventually *become* the successful people we want to be. Three key points will help: confidence, contacts, and caring.

CONFIDENCE COUNTS

When his church's minister of worship left to go to a new church, Rick thought he could easily step into her role. After all, he'd sung on the worship team for more than a year, his guitar-playing skills were pretty good, and he really felt called to build on the work that the previous worship leader had done. So the senior pastor gave Rick his approval to lead worship one Sunday morning.

Rick had most of the technical things down pat, but he lacked the confidence to stand up in front of the congregation and lead them in a truly meaningful worship experience. Because he *felt* awkward up there, he assumed everyone else *saw* how nervous he was. Embarrassed, he stumbled over his opening greeting and apologized more than once for not being as polished as his predecessor. For some reason, he actually apologized for not being as polished as Britney Spears!

Rick didn't seem to realize that the congregation wanted him to succeed. They would have been willing to overlook some first-time jitters. They simply wanted someone to lead them. By constantly drawing attention to his inexperience and his mistakes, though, Rick was actually telling his fellow church members that he wasn't up to the task, that he didn't feel strong enough to provide leadership. The congregation, in turn, responded by looking to other members of the worship team for leadership. Rick felt like a failure.

It's What You Do, Not How You Feel

If you find yourself in a new position—whether you're starting out in a new job or exploring a new career—you're naturally going to feel unsure of yourself in at least a few areas. That's fine. (In fact, your coworkers would probably think you're obnoxious if you thought you could move into a new job and immediately know everything!) But keep this fact in mind: Everyone likes to work with someone whom they see as being successful. Don't feel successful? Don't feel polished and self-assured? Don't trust your instincts? That's okay. Your *feelings* in these situations don't really matter. Act successful. Act polished and self-assured. Act as if your instincts are sound.

Just so there isn't any confusion about what I'm recommending, I'll share a personal example from the world of freelance writing.

Like most industries, freelance writing has written and unwritten rules. The written ones come in the form of "writers guidelines" that some magazines send out to potential contributors. They also come in articles for beginning writers that appear in magazines like *The Writer* and *Writer's Digest*. "If you want to succeed," they all suggest, "you've gotta follow these rules."

What isn't publicized, though, is that most of the rules apply only to beginners. Here's an example. Nearly all freelancers know that they're supposed to include a self-addressed stamped envelope (known as an SASE) whenever they send a proposal to an editor. That way, the thinking goes, the editor has an easy means for responding to the proposal, and you'll at least guarantee yourself a reply. If the editor has to scrounge around for an envelope, address it herself, and send it down to the mailroom, you might be waiting months for her answer. Or forever.

But this is what most of the pros know: The only thing to come in an SASE is a rejection letter. If the editor wants your article, he'll pick up the phone and call you so he can discuss the pay, length, and other details. Or nowadays, he'll send an e-mail, because it's faster and cheaper than mail. Instead of waiting around for the SASE to return like a homing pigeon, the pros pitch their ideas *without* an SASE, give the editor an appropriate amount of time to respond, follow up with an e-mail or phone call, and then move on. Therefore, including an SASE is often a signal to an editor that the writer is a beginner.

For some new and intermediate writers, the idea of not including an SASE is heresy. A sure path to Rejection City. Why? It goes against the rules. And if you go against the rules, you're going to fail.

This sounds plausible, but it's wrong. Articles don't get accepted because a writer follows rules. Articles get accepted because (1) the editor thinks the article will appeal to his readers (and won't offend the advertisers too much), (2) the editor has the budget to buy the article, and (3) the editor believes the writer has the ability to sit down and write the thing. Any number of prospective writers can make it past points one and two. But if an editor has the choice between working with someone who seems like a beginner and someone who has the confidence of a seasoned professional, I think the scales will tip toward the confident one.

You can't always get what you want
But if you try sometimes
You just might find
You get what you need.
—MICK JAGGER AND KEITH RICHARDS

Notice that I said "someone who has the confidence of a seasoned professional." I'm not talking about exaggerating past accomplishments. I'm not talking about trying to sound cocky or all-powerful in your interactions with other people. I'm simply talking about doing what confident people do— whether you actually *feel* that confident or not.

If you follow through, I believe you'll see immediate and long-lasting benefits. And eventually you will grow into your confidence, breaking it in like a comfortable pair of shoes.

Seeing the "Future You" Today

Many people never take the time to step back and create a specific mental image of what they want their career to look like. For a lot of years that was me: I just stumbled through my career, changing jobs when I got bored or the money and respect didn't seem sufficient, or the boss turned out to be—what's the word I'm searching for?—incompetent. I didn't have a clear picture of where I wanted to be. So, not surprisingly, the odds were against me ever actually getting there.

There is power in having a personal vision for where you want to go in your career and what kind of person you want to be along the way. Such a vision can play an incredibly important role in taking you from where you are today to where you want to go. So sit down. Stop and think about exactly what a successful someone in your chosen career is going to look like.

If you don't have any idea, you'll have some homework to do. You'll need to talk to people who are already at or near the career pinnacle you're aiming for. Maybe read the trade magazines for people in your chosen industry. If possible, attend a job fair, trade show, or association conference where you can meet and network with industry professionals.

You'll want to know how successful professionals in your industry dress, talk, and interact within the corporate hierarchy. Figure out how many hours they usually work and how well they treat the people who work for them.

What do they read? What conferences do they attend? What issues do they wrestle with?

Once you have a good idea of what a successful professional looks like in a given industry, ask yourself how you can acquire some of those traits. Notice I didn't say "all of those traits." Some won't fit your desired lifestyle or personal tastes. Some may even go against what you believe. That's fine. Absorb what you can. Discover which traits enrich and excite you, and set the rest aside. After all, you'll be bringing unique qualities of your own to every job you tackle. But emulating some of the success strategies of those who've gone before you will get you that much farther down the road, that much sooner.

MAKE GOOD CONTACTS

This section could be exactly two words long—*meet people*—but I'm getting paid by the word. (Just kidding. Don't editors *ever* laugh?)

We looked at the value of networking earlier in the context of learning about jobs, finding employment opportunities, and so on. I'd like to expand on that here and encourage you to take networking to the next level as a passionate employee.

So who are these people I'm suggesting you meet?

- coworkers
- supervisors/managers/bosses
- customers/vendors/suppliers
- colleagues in the industry

The first two categories—coworkers and supervisors, managers, and bosses—might sound like no-brainers. After all, how can you help meeting these people? They're the ones you're working with just about every Monday through Friday.

Maybe they are. But maybe not. It's easy to get so caught up in your own projects or the relationships within your own department—assuming you're in a company that has multiple departments—that you don't take the time to expand your horizons and build friendships with others throughout the company.

If you work in Marketing and have to occasionally stop by the Accounting department to nag them about something, nag nicely. Learn the names of the people in that area. It doesn't take long, and it won't negatively affect your work-day. But it will help you cement work relationships that may prove mutually beneficial in the future. If you ever need an accounting favor, the folks you've made an effort to get to know will be the ones willing to go the extra mile for you. On the other hand, if you treat them like "phone drones" who are there just to answer your calls and jump when you ask…well, don't be shocked if that "URGENT!!" request of yours just happens to accidentally find its way into a stack of coffee-stained papers waiting by the office recycling bin.

The Grapevine Effect

If you remain in the same type of business for a number of years, you'll also discover that your industry is a relatively small community. It's not unusual for people to move from company to company, position to position, and develop networking relationships that extend far beyond what you might expect. In-formation can spread throughout that network like lightning on caffeine. So can referrals. And so can the message: "You don't want to work with this guy." The more bridges you build between yourself and everyone else with whom you work, the better.

That also applies to customers, vendors, and suppliers and other colleagues who may work for related companies or even the competition. All of these groups can be links to new job opportunities that might interest you. Maybe they will also provide referrals for new business. Maybe they'll tip you off to professional development opportunities that can help you take your career to the next level. Even though I worked for publishing companies for many years, I didn't know much about the actual printing process until I had to work directly with a local four-color printer. He gave me a tour of his company and helped me understand the steps involved in turning a computer disk full of graphic information into a magazine.

If all of this "play nice, make friends" talk hurts your teeth, let me repeat a point from an earlier chapter: Just about everybody prefers working with someone they know rather than someone they don't know. The more people you know, the more people you can work with successfully. You never know where your current coworkers will end up in ten years. That shy woman who once worked in the cubicle next to yours might someday be in a position to

---

"I've Never Worked Harder"

My first job out of college was running the gift department for Kroch's & Brentano's bookstore in Oak Park, Illinois. I had taken the summer off to travel and had come home to find Real Life in front of me like a sheer cliff with no footholds. I might have found some entry-level white-collar job or training program if I had looked longer, but I had an overwhelming emotional need to be employed, immediately. I walked past Kroch's and saw "Help Wanted." I applied and got the job on the spot. (The manager was dazzled by my long list of favorite authors.)

The job had been vacant for a while and things were a mess, so I spent the first few weeks tidying and restocking the shelves. As Christmas approached I got to deck one of the display windows with little ceramic houses and fake snow. When the sales figures came in for December, gifts had quadrupled its revenues over the previous year. I thought of it as my first "A" in the Real World.

It may not have been an ideal career move, but I learned some useful things, such as how to be polite to people—no matter what. I also gained an appreciation of exactly how hard people work when they earn minimum wage. In a strictly physical sense, I've never worked harder.

—ELIZABETH GARDNER

hire you. Or give you a career-making lead. Or introduce you to the man or woman of your dreams. (Okay, that's not exactly career-related, but it's important nonetheless.)

Not every personal relationship you build is going to somehow "pay off" in work-related dividends. I'm not suggesting that you feign friendliness because it will benefit you down the road. I *am* suggesting that you expand your contacts by sincerely getting to know as many people around you as possible. Yes, sometimes those relationships will lead to work and career opportunities. And sometimes they won't. The worst that can happen? You'll just end up with more friends.

Careful with Those Matches!

One more thing about the importance of contacts: No matter what kind of company you work for, or what your chosen industry-of-the-moment happens to be, it's pretty much inevitable that you're going to run across people you just don't like or who just don't like you.

The temptation is to let them know how you feel. And if the obnoxious person happens to be your boss, the temptation is to tidy up that résumé, just so you can have the satisfaction of taking a new job, announcing to your current boss, "I quit!" and then relishing the act of telling him or her *exactly* what you think of their management style. Their office. Their hair color.

Don't.

Even if you *know* you will never again want to work for or near this particular person. Even if you think you have absolutely nothing to lose by burning this bridge. Even if you're moving across the country to join a monastery and vowing never again to speak aloud to another human being. Why? Because *you never know what the future might hold.* And the fleeting satisfaction of venting your feelings is just not worth it.

If you truly need to vent, vent to a trusted friend, a spouse, your pastor, a counselor.

If you want to take an action that is both symbolic and productive, vow to succeed like never before—either in the job you currently have or in a new one offering new opportunities. And if you just can't help yourself, send your former boss or coworker a nice e-mail thanking them for pushing you to discover this new part of yourself!

Show That You Care

I recently heard about a young temporary office worker who, during her first week in her first job, spent at least twenty minutes a day making personal phone calls. After a couple of days on the job, she showed up for work in jeans—ignoring the fact that everyone else was wearing business clothes. And then she decided she wanted to apply for a full-time position that was opening up in her department.

What do you think her chances were?

Yeah, zero.

But let's cut her a little slack, since it was her first job ever. How could she have known not to make twenty-minute personal phone calls? How was she supposed to know that this department didn't wear jeans or even observe "casual Friday"?

She could have asked. She could have paid attention to her coworkers. She could have laid low for a couple of weeks, gaining a sense of how the department operated, what the unspoken rules were, what responsibilities were expected of her as a member of the team. All of these actions would have sent the subtle message to her supervisors and coworkers that she cared about the job and her role in this particular workplace. And that would have helped solidify her place in the team.

Fitting into the corporate culture—without losing your own unique personality and point of view—helps smooth the way for pursuing your work to the best of your ability. If you show your sincere respect for the culture you're joining—by your actions, your appearance—you are more likely to receive the support of those who play an important part in maintaining that culture:

specifically, your supervisors and your coworkers. And if you have their support, you will also likely earn a measure of freedom to grow in your position and develop your passion for your work. They'll give you some leeway because you've shown that you care about the company and your place in the company. Finally, if you have the support of your supervisors and coworkers, you probably won't ruin things if you do occasionally make an office faux pas. (Not that I'd recommend going out of your way to put that to the test.)

I write this as someone who has always had a problem with corporate culture. I didn't like having a boss who told me when I should shave. I never liked having to wear a suit and tie to work. I also never had a lot of respect for companies that favored bureaucracy and hierarchies over actually *getting the work done* and meeting the needs of the customers. But I did recognize the fact that there is a line that must be walked if you want to remain within a given company. Maybe you can let your beard grow a little bit…if the boss sees you staying late to get ahead on an important project. Maybe it's okay occasionally to voice an opinion about the company's shortcomings…if you're also willing to suggest practical changes and work to implement them. It's all about balance. Knowing how to maintain that balance—which lines can be crossed and when it's appropriate to cross them—will come to you naturally if you truly do care about the company you work for and the people you work with. (The downside? If you *can't* care about the company you work for and the people you work with, start looking for another job. I don't think you can fake it.)

Fitting into the corporate culture is one important way to show that you care when you're on the job. But there are two more aspects of "show that you care" that can pay benefits in the future.

Invest Yourself

Think back to the Old Testament story of Moses that we looked at earlier. One of the points I made was that Moses simply discovered the burning bush that held the voice of God. He wasn't searching desperately for some sign of what he should be doing. He was just a guy out herding sheep. And then along came that bush. (Well, actually, the bush stayed where it was. Moses was the one who came along—followed, no doubt, by some weirded-out sheep.)

Now let's look at what happened next. God told Moses what he wanted him to do: "Go to Pharaoh and bring my people the Israelites out of Egypt." And Moses' winning response was:

"Huh? Me? You don't mean *me*."

"I do mean you. I'll be with you," God said.

"So, okay. I'm going to Pharaoh, and I'm all 'God sent me to deliver this message' or whatever. And he's going to be all 'Oh yeah? What's this God's name?' What am I supposed to say then?"

"Tell the Israelites, 'I AM has sent me to you.'"

Moses didn't even try to touch that one. Instead, he came back with more concerns: "What if they don't believe me? What if I don't say the right thing?" Then finally, "Lord, please send someone else." It's a wonder God didn't just say, "For crying out loud, Moses, give me a break!" Moses is acting like George McFly in *Back to the Future:* "What if I don't say the right thing? What if she doesn't like me? I don't think I could take that kind of rejection." At this point he's more geek than prophet. But God wasn't looking for a geek just then. He needed a leader, and he knew Moses was the man.

Why didn't Moses see that fact and just say, "Okay, God, I'll go to Pharaoh and I'll deliver your message"? Because he hadn't yet decided to invest himself in God's work. The reason was most likely a simple case of fear. Moses was probably scared to face Egypt's supreme ruler, scared to return to the land where he was a known murderer, scared to upset his calm life as a shepherd.

Business administration graduates are receiving lower starting salary offers than in the past, according to the National Association of Colleges and Employers. In 2002 salary offers dropped 7.1 percent from the previous year to $35,209.

And yet we all know, looking back, that Moses was absolutely born to do this job. He simply had to go through some challenging experiences before he was able to admit that to himself, commit to the job at hand, and show God that he truly cared.

Investing in your work involves more than just doing what's asked. Moses didn't just halfheartedly do what God said. He fought for the lives of the Israelites—he was their advocate—and he became intimately concerned with their deliverance. In the modern workplace, investing means caring enough about the job to interject your own ideas for improving a project, boosting revenues, improving customer service—whatever the case may be. It means recognizing that actions that benefit the company will likely benefit employees in the future and being willing to brainstorm solutions, put constructive comments in the suggestion box, form or serve on committees to solve internal problems, come up with fresh proposals and practical plans. Not every company recognizes its employees appropriately or rewards employee accomplishments. But I believe that those workers who take the time to invest themselves in their employers will reap the benefits.

Be Christlike in Your Attitude

If you are a Christian, one of the things you are probably passionate about is your faith. In fact, you may feel that you have the job you have and do the work you do specifically because God brought you to this place and gave you a specific calling. That's terrific. But please keep these three things in mind as you move through the workplace:

- Not everyone who is not a Christian is "bad."
- Not everyone who is a Christian is "good."
- Not everyone wants to be a Christian.

People in general come in "good" and "bad" and all of the flavors in between, regardless of what they profess to believe. There are Christians who are—forgive me if this offends you—jerks. And I've met many non-Christians who are wonderful people. And vice versa. Christian companies are not "heavenly"; they have just as many problems as non-Christian companies. And some non-Christian companies provide employment for an awful lot of committed believers.

Having a Christlike attitude toward coworkers means accepting them for who they are, flaws and all. It means not setting yourself apart from people because you have different spiritual beliefs. It means looking at people's hearts rather than their appearance. And it may mean listening to their hearts rather than tuning them out because they use words you choose not to say.

Throughout the Gospels, Jesus did all of these things when he encountered people in his journeys. He approached them as people, human beings, who had needs very much like his own. He met them where they were and explained where he was coming from. He knew he could offer them the gift of life, but he didn't force that gift on them. He allowed them to choose. Many did. Many refused. But he nevertheless continued to demonstrate his compassion for the world, all the way to the cross—and beyond.

I can't imagine a better example for showing care and passion on the job.

Chapter 7

Climbing the Corporate Ladder

In the 1920s and 1930s, the great stage magicians didn't have to make a fighter jet or the Statue of Liberty disappear in order to get people to applaud. They didn't need to divulge their colleagues' secrets or resort to movie-inspired special effects. They used the old, hokey tools of their trade to amaze their audiences with women who were sawn in two, mysterious floating balls, cut ropes that restored themselves, coins that seemed to multiply into millions, doves that appeared from the folds of a silk handkerchief.

And the old Indian Rope Trick.

In this one, a magician holding a coiled rope in his arms would walk out into a spotlight shining down onto an otherwise empty stage. A man, a rope, and a bare stage. What could be simpler? Then the magician would begin his "patter," the story he used to distract the audience's attention away from that leaky faucet at home, that work still sitting unfinished on a desk at the office, those myriad concerns and worries that threatened to draw the crowd away from the world of magic and drop them smack back into the real world. The patter helped the magician cast his spell.

In the case of the Indian Rope Trick, the patter always mentioned a miraculous event once witnessed in some anonymous marketplace in India long ago. I've forgotten a lot of the details, but they all revolved around a holy man who took his own coiled rope and tossed one end of it high into the sky, where it magically hung by itself, as if suspended from the clouds. Then a small boy plucked from the crowd would start to climb the rope. Higher and higher he'd go, until he literally disappeared into the clouds above. Then the rope would fall back to the earth. And the boy would leap out of a nearby basket, astounding the audience.

Or so the story goes.

And that's how the modern-day magician would have prepared his audience for his own version of the Indian Rope Trick. Maybe he would throw one end of the rope high into the hidden rafters of the auditorium stage, where it hung as if by—*gasp!*—magic. Maybe he would even dress up the trick a bit by laying the rope on the floor, picking up a small flute, and then playing a few hypnotic notes, encouraging the rope to rise into the air by itself, like a dazed cobra. Higher and higher it would rise, till it seemed to hang from the shadows of the ceiling. That's when the magician would stop, call for a young "volunteer" from the audience, and let "this young boy I have *never met before in my life*" climb up the stiffened rope and…vanish at the top, only to reappear at the back of the auditorium or among the audience. Or in a basket.

It's a cool trick. But I especially like the fact that it has some modern-day relevance for all of us who care about our careers.

Instead of a rope that disappears into the clouds, imagine a ladder. A *career* ladder. And instead of a young "volunteer" from the audience, imagine yourself climbing this ladder rung by rung, as everyone around you looks on in utter amazement. You're going higher. You're becoming more successful. Friends, loved ones, total strangers are applauding your accomplishments. Some will look at how high you're going and feel ashamed or embarrassed about their own humble place on their own ladders. And still you keep rising. Higher and higher and higher, until….

You disappear into the clouds.

The crowd of onlookers gasps as the ladder breaks apart and falls to the ground, scattering bits of wood and screws everywhere.

For a moment, everything is silent.

Then suddenly, you reappear among them. Right back where you started.

But now nobody is cheering. There is no applause to greet your amazing return. Just stunned silence.

The crowd can't believe it: The career ladder was just an illusion.

Onward, Upward...and Inward

The tough reality is that, like the Indian Rope Trick, the corporate ladder doesn't really lead anywhere you want to go. Companies close. Jobs disappear. Promotions may or may not occur. The things you love doing in your job may be the very things you have to give up if you're going to move up. I limited how high I could rise as a book editor because I didn't want to stop editing books, working with authors, and developing new manuscripts. All of the higher-ranking editors I knew spent their days attending meetings, developing budgets, and compiling reports for their bosses. That was not the life I wanted for myself.

What's money? A man is a success if he gets up in the morning and goes to bed at night and in-between does what he wants to do.

—Bob Dylan

One of the overriding assumptions of this book is that the job market shifted dramatically in the 1990s. Gone were the concepts of job security and employer benevolence. Replacing them were the ideas that workers are responsible for their own careers and that employers and employees owe each other nothing.

It may sound harsh, but this new attitude isn't all bad. Workers who leave their careers in the hands of employers—even the most conscientious and caring companies—risk disaster if those companies are forced into layoffs or closure. Like Bambi, their "parent" is suddenly ripped away from them, and they are left wide-eyed and helpless, riddled with self-doubt and feelings of abandonment. The more we take ownership of our careers, the better prepared we will be to weather whatever work-related storms we might have to face.

There's at least one major downside to this way of thinking. When we take ownership of our careers, it's easy to get carried away. We can become so self-absorbed that we turn into people whose chief concerns are, "What's in it for *me?* How will this help *me?* Why should I care about *that?*" We wind up managing our careers as if our life depended on it. But you know something? It doesn't. That's one of the fallacies of the career ladder. People who focus on the career ladder believe that their lives will only *really* be good/better/best if they reach this certain position in the company, if they earn this amount of money, if they put in this many hours, if they complete this list of goals.

The next time you're standing on a ladder, step up to the halfway point. Now, ask yourself what would happen if you were to step straight backwards. (If you try this at home, I'm not responsible for the results.) It doesn't take Isaac Newton to figure out that if you're halfway up a ladder and you take a step backwards, you're going to fall.

Most people think the results will be exactly the same if they step back from the career ladder. They'll fall. Their careers will shatter. And they'll have to start all over again on the bottom rung.

What they don't understand is that the only way to truly enjoy your career—to love what you're doing for the rest of your life—is to take that step of faith. It's exactly the kind of move that must be made if you find yourself focusing intently on working your way up the career ladder. You've got to step back. Step off. Take a long-distance look at where you are, where you've been, and where you seem to be going. Ask yourself, "Is this really what I want my life to be? Is this really what God wants me to be doing? Or have I been investing my time and energy in the wrong job, or even on the wrong approach to life?"

In her excellent small book *The Path,* Laurie Beth Jones writes,

As a child I had declared that my goal was to be able to make a living through my writing. With my ad agency I was indeed doing that. Yet one day after writing an ad for a hospital I felt so angry and frustrated that I tossed my copy across the desk. It wasn't that the ad copy wasn't good. The problem was that it was "good enough" to keep paying my bills, and thus allow me to continue to live in the shadow of my real dream.[1]

When she threw that crumpled ball of ad copy at the wall, Jones was taking a step off the career ladder. What's ironic is that it was a ladder she had built entirely herself. She had created her own highly successful ad agency, with clients throughout Texas and across the country. She took on the work she wanted to do and didn't have to live up to anyone's expectations but her own. Yet she still found herself focusing so intently on growing her agency and working her way up that she eventually lost sight of the real passions that had driven her so strongly in the beginning. Almost without realizing it, she'd gotten sidetracked in a career that was highly rewarding financially but that didn't feed her emotional and spiritual needs.

She stepped back. She risked falling and losing everything she had worked for. But holding tight to the career ladder and continuing her climb would have meant losing everything she most wanted in life. This is just what Jesus was talking about when he said, "What good is it for a man to gain the whole world, and yet lose or forfeit his very self?" (Luke 9:25). The answer is that it's *no* good.

Stepping back and taking stock is difficult when you're in the midst of building your career. The natural human tendency is to picture your journey up the career ladder as if it's a long steam train climbing a mountain with a limited amount of fuel. It's chugging along, inching its way up the incline—with its wheels screeching hard against the tracks and its smokestack pumping out thick white clouds of steam. Waste energy veering onto a side track? Bring the train to a dead stop halfway to the top? You'd have to be crazy. The sane approach is to keep steaming forward until you reach the summit. There will be plenty of time and energy for side trips and stops on the way down, once you're on the other side. For now, the top is all that matters.

In the workplace, though, there is no "top" for those whose primary goal is to climb the career ladder. They will never reach the point where "it's all downhill after this." They may work their way to the highest position within their company, but odds are that they will still feel personally unfulfilled. Or their spending habits will have risen along with their position, and a salary that once would have seemed astronomical is no longer enough to live on. So they look for other companies and better opportunities. And because the hunt for workplace fulfillment is still on, they never actually get around to stepping back and assessing the inner aspects of their career choices. They spend their entire careers living a life that's out of balance.

No Stress Here!

According to the 2002 *Jobs Rated Almanac*, the top five least-stressful jobs are:

1. Musical instrument repairer
2. Florist
3. Medical records technician
4. Actuary
5. Forklift operator

Don't think of stepping off the career ladder as a one-time event or something to be done only during a major turning point in your professional life. Instead, think about stepping back and taking stock with every forward step you take in your career. Make it a habit. That way you can virtually guarantee that you're doing exactly what you want to do, where you want to do it, to the best of your ability as both a productive working person and as a Christian.

Tools for the Trip

When it comes to travel, I like to prepare.

Before a trip to Belgium and France, I spent weeks with French phrase books and tapes, learning as much of the language as I could before my plane touched down. (Which basically amounted to the phrases "I am an American," "My name is Bob," and "Where is the bathroom?") Two months before my annual trip to New York City, I pull out my maps of the city streets and subway routes, review my restaurant guidebook, and refresh my knowledge of the city's landmarks. As a result, I actually know the streets of Manhattan better than the streets of the town where I've lived for the last ten years. Literally.

You don't have to plan to that extent to get the most out of your time "off the career ladder." But there are five main things you can focus on that will help you gain perspective, evaluate your current inward and outward success, and set goals for the future—whether you're reevaluating your current job, fresh in a new career, or simply curious about where your gifts and interests could possibly take you.

Give Yourself Time

A lot of us work for companies where "ASAP" is the rule of the day. Faster is always better. And a day that doesn't result in something tangible is a day wasted.

Get over it. Not all of us will need the same amount of time—and the time you need will certainly vary at different points in your life—but all of us need *some* time to let the immediate demands of the job fade from our minds and find the mental space to think clearly. To use a Manhattan analogy, it's like going from the crush and bustle of Times Square—a tourist destination and business center packed with people and traffic—to a quiet boat on a pond in

Central Park. You can't get from one place to another in the blink of an eye. It takes time. And it takes patience.

In *Rolling Nowhere,* Ted Conover writes about the time he spent trying out life "riding the rails" as a hobo. He was really a pretty well-off college student. But he needed a break, he was intrigued by human nature, and he was curious about the lives of these men on the outskirts of society. After only three days, though, he discovered something important about himself and about the hobo way of life:

> I was in a hurry to meet some hoboes, and in a hurry to learn how to
> ride the rails like a pro. But the rails were not meant for people in a
> hurry. My summer had been a time of appointments, prearranged meet-

---

"What If I Pay You to Let Me Work?"

I moved to San Francisco a few months after my sixteenth birthday and started job hunting with zero skills—just my high-school diploma and one quarter of college under my belt, but nothing that helped me on a job application.

I read the want ads religiously and applied for everything I thought I might be able to do. How about being a clerk at Woolworth's Department Store? Sorry, kid, you need experience before we can hire you. But how can I get experience if nobody will hire me? Can't help you, kid. Lunch-counter job? Sorry. Busgirl? Can't use you. Janitor? Nope. *Any* job, doing *any*thing? Sorry, you have to have some experience to work for us. Would you let me work for you a week without pay so I can show you I can do the job? Sorry, kid.

Pretty soon I was offering to work two weeks for free, then three, then a month. But nobody was interested. Finally I stopped into a diner that had a "Waitress Wanted" sign in the window. The manager looked me over, asked my age, and said, "Well, I guess we could use you." He told me what I'd have to wear and said I'd have to go buy

ings, bus and plane schedules, and telephone calls, all efficiently squeezed into as little time as possible. Time was money, and idle moments were wasted moments. On the rails, though, that was not the point. Here one was not a productive unit—hardly a part of the economy at all, in fact— and life was more attuned to watching, thinking, and talking.[2]

However you find it, wherever you spend it, this is the kind of time you need.

Read for Refreshment

In most jobs, there's lots of reading material to sift through. Newsletters, product announcements, training manuals, employee handbooks, trade magazines,

---

a pair of white waitress shoes like the ones the other girls were wearing. "Be here at 9:00 Monday, and we'll show you the ropes," he said. I was thrilled. At last, a real job!

Monday morning, full of optimism and determination to make good, I show up at the diner at a quarter to nine. It's closed. Closed? How could it be closed? I waited. 9:00, still closed. 9:30, 10:00, 10:30…still closed. Then I learned that the place wasn't just closed for the day, it was closed permanently. Turned out the manager knew it would be closed Monday when he gave me the "job" that Friday.

Back to pounding the pavement.

After a total of three months of knocking on doors, pleading for *any* job, no matter what, anything at all just to get started, I saw an ad offering a hostess job at a Sizzler Steak House in San Mateo. *I can do that,* I thought, so off I went. And I got the job.

The work was hard. But before I moved on, I learned all the jobs in the store (other than manager): from dishwasher to cleaner to cook to cashier. I learned how fun it was to turn a sour customer into a smiler. And…well, I still have a soft spot for Sizzlers.

—Peggy J. Noonan

and on and on. In an effort to budget our time, we develop a knack for weeding out all of the superfluous stuff and focusing our attention on the words that really matter. Sometimes these habits carry over into our off-hours as well.

Men, especially, are notorious for reading only the most practical material. Many of us can't be bothered with novels or general-interest magazines or biographies. We want the stuff that's going to have immediate, measurable results in our lives. And by "lives," we usually mean "business lives." That's why we see such a flood of books tied to management principles, success strategies of major-corporation CEOs, and even discussions of the business advice to be gleaned from Attila the Hun.

According to the National Labor Relations Act of 1935, it's illegal to punish people for revealing their wages to one another.

If you're just starting out in the work world, it's easy to get caught up in all of this. There are so many useful theories out there, so many great psychological insights, so many negotiation and planning strategies hidden between the covers of hundreds of business books and journals—and many of them can truly help you achieve better results and be more effective in your chosen career. That's not even counting the basic, essential information you can pick up from reading the trade magazines and newsletters aimed at the professionals in your chosen line of work. (Every imaginable industry has them.)

If you constantly spend your off-hours with reading material like this, though, you're going to burn yourself out. Yes, you might become a walking encyclopedia of industry information. You might be able to recite product codes or customer phone numbers in your sleep. But you'll also likely reach the point at which such immersion in business information will be counter-productive. It's not that the human brain can't hold all of this information. It can. But it needs to expand and grow in other areas, too. It needs quiet time to discover a variety of subjects. In fact, making time for true leisure reading can actually help your brain make important—and serendipitous—connections between otherwise dissimilar things, connections that can directly lead to product and service innovations, creative thinking, and significantly more interesting conversation around the coffee machine.

Here's the strategy that has worked for me: Start by picking a different kind of reading material. Never touch daily newspapers? Buy a paper—and read at least the first paragraph of every article. Don't usually read fiction? Pick up a novel. Love books? Try a couple of magazines.

Next, shake things up a little bit more by exploring new territory. If you don't want to suddenly switch from Salon.com to Elizabethan poetry, or to go from the *Wall Street Journal* to Stephen King, look for books that combine your current passions with a new, refreshing format. If you love mysteries, try a true-crime book by Ann Rule. If you immerse yourself in work-related material about hotel management, seek out novels set in hotels. If you only read books from Christian bookstores or your church library, try Christian-themed books you might have overlooked: Jan Karon's "Mitford" novels, for example, or Laurie Beth Jones's business-minded nonfiction *The Path* and *Jesus, CEO*. And if you're at a total loss about where to start, go to Barnes & Noble's Web site (www.bn.com) or Amazon.com, look up a book you have read and enjoyed, and look for headings on the page like "If you liked this, then try…" or "Readers who bought this book also purchased…" Sure, you may end up finding books that are quite different from your original selection. You also may end up enjoying them.

Remember: I'm not suggesting that you run out and start a book club. Or that you spend every free moment reading something. Just take the time to step back from your usual routine and discover something new. In the process, I believe your outlook on both life and work will be refreshed.

Seek Others' Opinions

Not that long ago, as a result of some work frustrations and life crises, I went through a period when I had to step away and assess where I was and what I was experiencing.

I hesitated when it came to making my feelings known to my friends and colleagues, though. It's hard to be vulnerable, to honestly open yourself up to criticism and others' possible judgmental attitudes. Yet that seems to be the only way to really get the help that can give you insight into your situation. It's also a great way to be reminded just how many friends you do have.

Many of life's failures are people who did not realize how close they were to success when they gave up.

—THOMAS EDISON

Set aside whatever public persona you may have put on, let down your guard, and ask what others think about your situation. In response to a note I posted on a subscribers-only discussion list for writers, I received dozens of supportive e-mails. And I heard from a lot of people who said, basically, "I've been feeling this way too, but I thought I was the only one." I'm sure my frustration was relatively short-lived because I made the effort to share my feelings with others who could relate. It helped just to get my feelings "out there," in the world at large.

You're not the only one. You don't have to make decisions all alone. Friends and loved ones can give you a fresh perspective. They can see things in you and in your life that you've overlooked. They may even know what you're feeling before you recognize it yourself.

So talk with people you trust, who know you and understand your values. You have much to gain.

Write Your Journey

This is one of those "do as I say, not as I do" things. I've never been good at keeping a journal or a diary. On the rare occasions when I've done so, I've enjoyed going back years later and reading through everything. And I always say to myself, "Ah, why didn't I write even more? Why didn't I make this a habit? There's so much I didn't bother to get down on paper." So I appreciate journals after the fact. But it's like pulling teeth to get me to sit down and actually maintain one on a daily basis. (Maybe it's because I write for a living; my skin crawls at the thought of writing five hundred or one thousand words every day and not getting paid for it.)

On the other hand, if you can make the time to sit down and "think aloud on paper," you may find that journaling is a valuable way to chart your thoughts about your work and what it means to you as a human being. Bible verses, significant quotes, "pros" and "cons" columns, prayers, song lyrics—a wide variety of things can make up the text of your journal. And you can be as honest and unguarded as you want, since no one but you has to see what you've written.

An additional benefit of having a written record of your growth: You can go back in a couple of years and see just how God was working in your life at every step along the way.

Pray

God *is* working in your life. But maybe he'd like to do even more in your life than you're currently allowing him to do. Maybe he's trying to clue you in to a new direction or a new relationship. Maybe there are some things in your life that he'd like to change. Everything that God wants to do for you can happen more easily, more deeply, if you open yourself up to his leading through prayer.

THREE QUESTIONS

In the old romantic comedy *Pat and Mike,* Pat (a woman) is an amateur athlete who is good—if not excellent—at just about every major sport, and Mike (a man) is the borderline-sleazy sports manager who wants to take her under his wing, help her go professional, and hopefully, make some good money for himself in the process.

Pat's flattered by his confidence in her abilities, but she's also more than a little put off by the rules he imposes on her, since she's "in training": an early bedtime, no smoking, no dating, and no "bad" food. She's also annoyed by the way Mike treats one of his other clients, a young and not-very-successful boxer named Hucko. Whenever Hucko starts thinking that Mike's being too hard on him or that he'd be better off on his own or with another manager, Mike stops him and makes him repeat the answers to "the three questions":

"Who made ya, Hucko?"

"You, Mike," the boxer says with a defeated shrug.

"Who owns the biggest piece of ya?"

"You, Mike."

"What'll happen if I drop you?"

"I'll go right down da drain, Mike."

"And?" Mike presses.

"And stay dere."

For Hucko the boxer, those three questions define the scope of his relationship with Mike and, by extension, the relationships Mike will allow him to have with everyone else. As you step back and take a look at your relationship to work and career, you can get a pretty good feeling for where things stand by asking yourself three questions of your own:

- Do I enjoy what I'm doing?
- Am I earning enough to meet my needs (not wants)?
- Am I making a difference?

Do you look forward to going to work? Is work fun for you? Are you satisfied with how your talents and interests come together in your job? Do you like your place in the organization or your role in the industry?

Is your job paying you enough to live on and care for the basic needs of food, clothing, shelter? Is it paying enough to also meet future retirement needs? medical and dental needs?

Are you earning too much? That may sound utterly ludicrous to you, but we tend to match our spending to our income; if you're earning far more than you need to live on, your money may be leading you in some wrong directions in terms of your overall emotional and spiritual well-being. If you are earning more than you can handle wisely, you may already be feeling the negative effects of a lifestyle too bound up with possessions and appearances.

Finally, are you contributing something to society or your profession or your community? If you feel that the answer is no, that doesn't mean you should quit your job today and step out into something entirely new. It may mean you need to change the way you do your job or that you simply need to adjust your attitude toward your work.

There are no right or wrong answers that apply to everyone. What is right and meaningful for your neighbor may be wrong for you. But the important thing is to take the time, make the effort, and give your spot on the career ladder some serious thought. In return you'll discover the insight you need to guide yourself toward success and appropriately handle any of the hurdles and headaches that life will throw at your career.

Chapter 8

Handling On-the-Job Hurdles

There's no question about it: Some days the career glass is full to overflowing. Other days, it's just half full. And on still other days, you can turn that glass upside down, give it a violent shake, and *still* not get it to give up even a single drop. Bone dry.

No matter how much you love your job, you're going to have some bone-dry days.

Sometimes you're just not in the mood for work. I can't tell you how many gray, rainy days I wished I could avoid the commute to work and stay home, pop a movie in the VCR, and just chill. We all hit cycles when we can't keep our mind on our work, or we simply don't feel like going to the office, for whatever reason. Still, we keep showing up. Because the alternative means losing pay, maybe even losing our job.

All of us will experience other downtimes, though, that are more serious, when we confront hurdles at work that make losing our job not all that unappealing. The work may not have changed, but other issues have arisen that ended up sucking all the fun out of it.

Maybe staff changes have left you with significantly more work than you can handle—and a management team that can't understand that fact.

Maybe a boss you liked and respected has been replaced by someone with less experience than you but a lot more authority. (That's a dangerous combination, in case you were wondering.)

Maybe your job description has changed, and you're suddenly responsible for overseeing processes or projects you don't quite understand. You feel as if you're floundering.

Maybe you'd love to work your way up…but there's nowhere "up" to go.

That's the situation Jill Donaldson faced. She was a talented advertising account executive who attracted new clients to her agency, presented her own campaigns to clients, and was earning good money. But it was a small, family-owned company. And even though she was eager to work her way up and take on greater responsibility, that just wasn't possible. The owner and his son occupied the two top slots—and there wasn't any room left for "outsiders," no matter how capable they might be. Jill loved her job and loved the idea of working with a small company. But she eventually had to face her hurdle head-on and make a tough career choice. She could stay and stagnate, or she could start moving forward. Not too surprisingly, she chose to leave.

From Bill Gates to Bill the janitor, every working person will eventually have to confront on-the-job hurdles that range from little to life changing. But knowing they're coming—and knowing how you'll handle them when they do appear—can give you the confidence boost needed to keep your career on track.

A Rude Awakening

When Beth Cooney took her first job out of college as a newspaper reporter, she struggled to make the transition from student to employee. "I was still very much into my college lifestyle," she says. She was more focused on planning weekends with her friends at Cape Cod and enjoying the nightlife than actually taking responsibility in her new job. Eventually her boss called her into his office and threatened to fire her if she didn't get her act together.

"You are potentially a very good reporter," he told her. "But you're not willing to work as hard as somebody in this business needs to work." He was right. Beth was used to leaving work after her eight hours, whether her stories were finished or not. "That's not how it works in this business," she was told.

How did Beth handle her boss's reprimand?

"I walked out, went into the bathroom, and threw up," she says.

(Thanks for sharing, Beth.)

But she didn't want to get fired. So she took steps to change. "I started to work like a slave. I was there day and night, putting in sixty or seventy hours a week," she says. "My goal was to get my stories on the front page every day." And all of that extra work paid off. Her stories were hitting the front page regularly. Even better, those stories were having an impact on her community. Her reporting was suddenly making a real difference in people's lives. It was also becoming more meaningful for Beth herself.

In 2000 there were roughly 681,000 lawyers, 217,000 pharmacists, and 71,000 radio and TV announcers working in the United States.

Today she says she owes that first editor a lot. "I hadn't been prepared to work at a daily newspaper when I walked in the door. They were giving me a reality check about the business: 'If you want to do this, this is what it takes.'"

That's a tough thing to hear. Early in my own career, my reaction to such criticism was to run away, figuring that I must not be in the right job or else everything would be perfect. Well, no job is *perfect* all the time. And sometimes getting a reality check about just what needs to be done can be the best thing to happen. Even though it might feel like a pitcher of ice water in the face.

This Isn't What I Thought It Would Be

Beth had to face the fact that her *idea* of what a reporter's job should be didn't mesh with the *reality* of working in a newsroom. If you're just taking your first full-time job, it's only natural to expect similar culture shock at the outset. And why not? You've never done this before. How are you supposed to know what to expect?

Well…

Actually, there are several steps you can take to minimize this hurdle before it looms up in the middle of your career path.

1. *Talk to other people who do what you're doing.* If Beth had taken the initiative to talk to working reporters earlier on in her employment—or even prior to accepting the job—she could have avoided the confrontation with her boss.

2. *Compare your work style to that of your coworkers.* Are your coworkers all staying until six even when your official hours end at five? If so, ask them why. If their work situation is similar to yours, you may need to be putting in more time than the "official" minimum. (If you ask around and find out that you're putting in significantly *more* time or effort than your colleagues, you will have to decide whether it would be appropriate for you to scale back—and perhaps risk your standing in the company—or whether you just happen to be surrounded by a bunch of slackers.)

3. *Read about your job.* I'm convinced that absolutely every industry and every possible occupation known to humanity is supported by a trade organization. And I think every one of them publishes either a magazine or a newsletter that can provide valuable tips about how people do jobs just like yours. If none of your coworkers can point you to the right material, though (and that's seriously unlikely), drop by the nearest good-size public library and look for the *Encyclopedia of Associations* in the reference section. It's a multi-volume set that lists every association imaginable—and a lot that aren't—and describes what publications those groups produce. Then it's a matter of calling or writing to the groups and requesting a copy (or ordering a subscription). But remember, this is a worst-case scenario. If you're working in an office, your in-box will

probably receive regular deliveries of industry-related and job-related periodicals. You almost certainly won't have to go looking for reading material.

4. *Get training.* Sometimes "This isn't what I thought it would be" actually means "I feel totally baffled and/or confused about this job." If that's you, don't feel ashamed. And don't wait for someone to notice. Go to your supervisor and ask for additional training to help you understand every facet of your job. If your boss explains that there "just isn't any money in the budget for training," you could type your fingers blue finding resource after resource on the Internet that supports the premise that more training results in a better financial return for the company. In other words, training helps companies *make* money. So be prepared to argue your case (politely) and support your desire with real facts about your own job and your expectation for improved efficiency, effectiveness, customer service, whatever as a result of your newly acquired skills.

What you don't need to mention is that more training will also give you increased confidence and will probably give you a lot more pleasure in doing your job. It may also help your chances for future promotions and raises.

Coworker Clashes

Ever watch reruns of the old *Dick Van Dyke Show* on Nickelodeon? If you haven't seen it, it's about Rob Petrie (played by Dick Van Dyke), his life at home (with a wife, played by Mary Tyler Moore, and an annoying—to me—son), and his life at the office, where he spends his days as one of three writers for a TV comedy show. In my opinion, it's one of the funniest old TV shows around. And because it focuses so much on Rob's life at the office, it's a great antidote to present-day work frustrations. Because everybody usually gets along. There isn't any gossip. It's a fun, creative working environment where jokes and fast wit are not only valued, they're rewarded.

If that sounds like your work life, consider yourself fortunate.

Most people *don't* find themselves working in mutually supportive teams, in offices where there's no gossip and no politics. For most people, coworker conflicts are as much a part of daily work life as a ringing telephone.

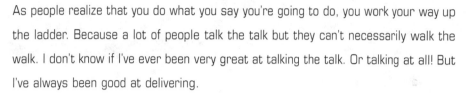

As people realize that you do what you say you're going to do, you work your way up the ladder. Because a lot of people talk the talk but they can't necessarily walk the walk. I don't know if I've ever been very great at talking the talk. Or talking at all! But I've always been good at delivering.

—Jerry Bruckheimer

If you haven't yet encountered this, don't be discouraged—you will. But that shouldn't be a hurdle that has to keep you from enjoying the company you work for and loving your job. If you know at the outset that many, many employees gain great pleasure from talking about their coworkers or dirtying others' reputations or backstabbing to get what and where they want, you'll be ready to deal constructively with these situations when they do arise. Real life may not be the *Dick Van Dyke Show* or even *Just Shoot Me*—in fact, at your job it may be a lot more like *Survivor* or *Fear Factor*—but that doesn't mean you can't still work to make your part of the company a fun, friendly place, *despite* the interpersonal problems that can occur.

Playing Politics

There's a reason why "politician" is low on the list of respected professions (placing 250th out of 250 possible professions in one survey): Politicians seem manipulative, two-faced, and downright slimy. Why, then, do so many of us choose to "play politics" at the office?

For most of us, playing politics means being false in order to manipulate other people to achieve our goals. And in a work environment, there's no escaping it. However, that doesn't mean you have to participate in political games.

Consultant Ken Lawson notes that the best way to approach office politics is to "figure out what people are really looking for and, without compromising yourself or your own needs, give it to them."[1]

The following five steps can help you put office politics into perspective and develop positive, helpful relationships in the workplace:

1. Work at developing strong professional relationships at your current place of employment.
2. Play nice. In other words, be willing to share what you know with others.
3. Be open to different styles of work and different kinds of personalities in the workplace.
4. Be flexible when it comes to matching your own personality and work habits with others' personal preferences.
5. Fit in; don't stand apart.

For Christians, the idea that we should "be flexible" and "open," that we should work to "fit in," may be difficult to understand. We're used to the idea of the lone Christian fish swimming against the world's currents, the fish that *doesn't* try to fit in or go with the flow. Doesn't fitting in mean compromising who we are as believers?

Biblically speaking, we are called by God to stand apart, to be salt and light for the world. But unfortunately, the Bible isn't able to give us a clear-cut look at life in the modern workplace. There really aren't too many accurate parallels we can draw between Jesus' "working life" with the disciples and our job at the bank, factory, or office. We're separated by two thousand years of history and light-years of cultural experiences.

If you find yourself in doubt about just how far you need to stretch in order to fit in with others and avoid interpersonal conflicts, ask yourself what positive steps you can take that would allow you to better mesh with your coworkers and supervisors *without compromising who you are as a person and as a Christian.* Can you turn down the volume of the CD playing in your cubicle? Sure you can. Can you join your coworkers at the company picnic—even though you personally voted for an on-site company Fun Fair? Absolutely. Can you go along with the company's decision not to decorate the offices at Christmas, for fear of offending those employees who don't celebrate Christmas? Well…maybe you can, maybe you can't, but it's worth considering all the factors involved in your decision.

How you respond to office politics can have a direct impact on your long-term success in your career.

"They Needed a Know-Nothing Program Director"

I was eighteen and had just graduated from broadcasting school when I got my first full-time job at a country-music radio station. I was on my way!

The job was receptionist/"traffic girl" as we were known in those days. "Traffic" meant scheduling commercials—a tedious, detail-oriented chore that I heartily disliked. A week after I started work, the general manager promoted me to program director—with no raise in pay or evidence of ability. I couldn't understand why he wanted me in the job, but I couldn't say no. After all, it meant getting out of doing traffic and moving into a nice office, where I soon found myself twiddling my thumbs.

I took the initiative a couple of times and tried to be a good PD, but the general manager angrily told me to go back to my office and twiddle. After a few months, I quit.

I called the station a year or two later to say hi to former coworkers and found out that the general manager and the bookkeeper had been caught embezzling and were sent to jail. Apparently they needed a know-nothing PD around who wouldn't figure out their game!

—LaVonne Ellis

Management Mayhem and Corporate Conflicts

I recently heard from a college-student friend, we'll call her Traci Steffen, who found herself in an unusually awkward work situation. Traci had just finished her junior year at a university in Missouri—studying business and journalism—when she snagged a summer job closer to her family back in Kansas as a newsletter editor/writer. But "snagged" is the key word. Once she accepted the job, the situation didn't take long to fall apart. Traci told me:

> The boss hired me as an intern and offered to pay my room and board in a condo and give me a small stipend. At that time, though, she was living in the condo and was also publishing her health and fitness newsletter from offices there. She said she was moving the offices out, and I would then be able to have the place to myself. Once it got closer to the date, though, she called me and said she didn't have the money to secure the new offices—and that she and I and the publication would all be sharing space in the same condo. I could have turned down the internship at that point, but I had already turned down all my other options. I didn't feel like I had any choice.
>
> It wasn't that bad for a while. As time progressed I think she became frustrated with living with me and my lifestyle. I would stay out late with my friends, but I would always be at my desk working on time. Not once was I late. I was just really lonely, and I felt like I needed to be with my friends instead of being home with her.
>
> We had some talks about it. I said I felt stifled working at a job in the same place where I lived. She also always made me feel as if I was not working fast enough or doing work that was good enough for her. At times I felt like I was just manual labor. In the end she told me she was running out of money. I surely believe it because by that point she was living on hot dogs (five packs for one dollar), and the other editor

in the office—yes, there were three of us working in that condo!—was
bringing in her own toilet paper.

So I had to leave.

My problem is that I have this company listed on my résumé. It
was a big job and I did a LOT of work for them. I am afraid, however,
that when I start applying for staff positions, my prospective employers
are going to call the company even if I don't list it as a reference. I am
torn between leaving that experience on my résumé or taking it off. I
don't know which would be worse in the long run. If some employer
did ask me why I didn't want that company to be contacted, I would
most definitely explain the entire situation. Working with my boss
there was a perfect example of a double bind.

Trust Your Gut

There were any number of warning signs in Traci's situation. In fact, she might
have been suspicious about the arrangement from the very start, from the
boss's offer to pay her room and board in a condo. "Well, why not just pay me
a reasonable wage," Traci could have said, "and I'll find my own place to live."
Also, the boss's promise that she'd be moving the newsletter's offices out of the
condo "eventually" might have sent red flags scurrying up the flagpole. "What
does 'eventually' really mean?" Traci could have asked. Or better: "Could we
put something in writing about that?"

Traci's an incredibly savvy young woman. In fact, she has taken charge of
her education, networking relationships, and career opportunities to a greater
extent than anyone else I know, period. I fully expect her to become a brilliantly successful entrepreneur. But in this case, I think her gut was telling her
one thing, but logic was telling her something else. She probably should have
trusted her gut.

When her boss called to change the terms of their deal, Traci knew it
sounded bad but she didn't believe she had any options. And besides, this paid
internship was going to give her real-world experience in her major and put

her closer to family and friends. Those benefits proved more compelling than that gnawing feeling of doubt in her stomach.

Writer Margaret Littman was talking with me about freelance writing assignments when she made these comments, but I think they apply to every job situation:

> Go with your gut. If a project seems like it is going to be too much work for too little money, if it seems the boss doesn't know what he or she wants, if you suspect you will be thinking about poking your eye out with a fork before it is over, say no. In ten years doing this, my gut has never failed me. Except when I have ignored it.

Just as you know when you really shouldn't be walking alone down a dark street, you'll have a sense of whether a particular job "opportunity" is in your best interest or is a disaster waiting to happen.

When the Boss Is a Jerk

Some people are afraid to speak the truth honestly. I don't know if they prefer to see the world through rose-tinted glasses, where everything looks delicate and beautiful, or if they just don't want to seem bitter or spiteful or mean. Whatever the case, if you find yourself tempted to tiptoe around the truth of your workplace situation, let me encourage you to put both feet firmly on the floor—and maybe even do some stomping. Because the fact is that some

People who define themselves largely by their jobs are relying on an exterior frame of reference to tell them what they are worth. A healthy attitude toward work results from healthy self-esteem, not the other way around.

—Joanne Cleaver

bosses are going to act like jerks. (If "jerks" offends you, substitute "bullies," "dictators," "fascists," "idiots," "ignoramuses," or something similar.)

I'm not suggesting this is how you should *talk* about your boss or your supervisors in the workplace. I'm also not recommending after-hours gossip or name-calling. I'm talking about your boss's attitude toward you and your work—and your ability to recognize when someone in a position of authority has crossed the line. Some bosses believe that they motivate by intimidation, coercion, and threats. Some think that you'll work harder or better if they yell. Some lack any sense of where their "bossdom" ends and your private life begins. They don't demonstrate respect for you or your work.

I once worked for a division of a Christian publishing company that was overseen by someone I would definitely put in the "jerk" category. At the time, we also attended the same church and sat on the same deacon board.

If you were to see Bruce (not his real name) solely at church, you would be impressed. He was apparently a loving father, a devoted husband, and a thoughtful leader. But if you were to sit in a meeting with him at work, you'd discover a different side to the man. He was imperious, condescending, and unreasonably demanding of his staff.

Early on I was far enough down the corporate ladder that I didn't have to endure that side of Bruce too often. Then my boss's boss quit. After that my immediate boss left as well. And soon the corporate reporting hierarchy stretched straight from Bruce to me. Yippee.

I hadn't enjoyed working for this company for some time. I was mentally on my way out. But one of the final straws came on a Sunday morning at church. At that particular church the deacons were responsible for distributing the communion "wine" (grape juice) and "bread" (tiny crackers). As we deacons were all lining up in the church vestibule, waiting for the pastor to finish his prayer so we could process to the front altar and pick up our communion trays, Bruce leaned over to me and said, "So how is that big project coming? You going to be done on time?"

For my money, this stands out as the crowning example of jerkdom.

So what's a mere worker to do?

The easiest but probably the least satisfying solution is to quit. "Easiest" because you'll be immediately free of the offending boss. "Least satisfying," though, because you won't have developed the skills to help you deal constructively with the next bullying boss. Before you even think about taking the serious step of quitting, try to focus on the positive aspects of your job and keep the following four points in mind:

1. *Don't take it personally.* In fact, the more upset your boss gets, the more you should sympathize with him. At the same time, don't just blow off everything a "jerky" boss says; you may find the boss's approach or attitude offensive, but that doesn't mean the points he's making aren't valid. However, if tirades and personal attacks become a regular part of your workday, it's time to walk away— either to another department or another company. You are a valuable, worthwhile person who deserves respect in the workplace. Don't be ashamed to stand up for yourself.

2. *Keep your boss informed.* Some bosses act like bullies because *their* bosses are on their backs. One of the ways you can help is to make sure your immediate supervisor is up to date on your projects, any problems you might be having, and so on. Open lines of communication—through e-mail or just walking down the hall for a daily chat—can go a long way toward building bridges.

3. *Try to accept your boss for who she is.* Frankly, everybody is dealing with something. Your boss may be experiencing problems with her own job, difficulties at home, or even serious personal problems that you can't know—or do—anything about. Work at accepting and understanding, but don't assume that you can always "fix" a bad situation.

4. *Pray for your boss.* Praying for those who seem bent on persecuting you can be one of the hardest things to do. Yet it can bring positive results. People and situations can change as a result of your prayers.

And you may also find that *you* change for the better as a result of praying for your boss.

Handling Upheaval

This morning's paper carried a number of stories that are fairly typical of our current business climate:

- "Kmart Corp. is preparing to sell two of its six corporate jets." This, following months of layoffs and hundreds of store closings.
- "Employees of Granger Container Services"—a local waste-collection company—"might unionize this week."
- "The state's largest processor of Michigan-grown apples has filed for Chapter 11 bankruptcy protection."
- "Ex–Arthur Andersen partner obstructed justice…says he knew he was breaking the law when he directed other employees to follow policies that led to the shredding of Enron Corp.–related documents."

Job interviews can be tough. But some companies make them tougher than they have a right to, asking questions that are not legally allowed. It probably won't help your employment chances to whip out your cell phone and call 911 if one of the following questions comes up during an interview. It *might* help, though, if you're prepared with a professional, diplomatic response…just in case.

Employers cannot legally ask your

- marital status, or whether a female applicant is pregnant or planning to become pregnant;
- racial, ethnic, or national background;
- sexual orientation;
- political affiliations or religious beliefs; or
- age, unless you're under eighteen.

Local, national, and international companies regularly experience changes that can alter the personality and work environment of an organization and lead to increasing anxiety, stress, and fear about the future for its employees.

Economic downturns lead to layoffs, permanent downsizing, or restructuring that puts more work and more responsibility on your desk—with no corresponding "more" in your paycheck.

Companies decide they can do business more efficiently or more cheaply in another location, and you can do nothing to stop your livelihood from moving to another city, another state, another country.

Companies get caught up in scandal—crucial parts that failed, leaders who lied, accountants who cheated—and you are powerless to change the fact that a once-respected organization is now, incredibly, a dark stain on your résumé.

New leadership takes over and "cleans house," and suddenly the old managers are gone and all of the key slots are filled with the boss's friends.

Bad things happen to good companies, and it's usually the employees (and often the customers) who end up paying the price. The effects on you may be dramatic—a day that begins like any other but ends with you being escorted to your car, carrying a box containing the contents of your now-former desk—or they may be slow and subtle—an increasingly thickening atmosphere of cynicism, a pervasive sense of anxiety and despair. No matter why the change has occurred or what its ultimate impact will be on you and your job, you must face up to its effects on you emotionally, psychologically, and spiritually. To dismiss or ignore them can prove even worse in the long run. Here are some things you can do to cope with such upheavals:

- *Talk with someone outside the situation.* If you talk only to coworkers and colleagues who are stuck in the same troubling environment, you may begin to feel overwhelmed and helpless. So talk with someone who can give you a fresh perspective: a pastor, a close (nonwork) friend, a counselor or therapist. You may be surprised at how good it can feel to simply discuss your experience with an objective listener.

- *Put your own house in order.* No matter what may be going on around you, do your best to keep doing your best. Meet deadlines. Contribute during meetings. Continue to give your job as much energy and attention as you can.

- *Work to maintain your sense of humor.* Anxiety and fear can increase exponentially when the "bad situation" is all employees can think and talk about. Inject even a small fraction of genuine laughter, and you can play a significant part in dispelling others' worries while alleviating your own stress.

- *Polish up that résumé.* If the company is truly sinking—or even if it's deteriorating to the point where you don't want to stay anymore, even if it manages, somehow, to stay afloat—give serious thought to moving on. This can be even harder than it sounds. I've found it especially challenging to devote myself to my job with a "sinking ship" while also trying to put on my best business smile and confidently market my skills elsewhere. An oppressive atmosphere of uncertainty and anxiety tends to drain away your confidence and trust, and that's not the ideal condition in which to enter a job interview with another company. If this is the kind of situation you're in, work to maintain a solid support network of encouraging family and friends outside the company. These are the people who will affirm your abilities and applaud your efforts to find a healthier, happier work environment.

There's no getting around the fact that, at times, even your perfect job will feel more like work and less like fun. But once you know the hurdles that can arise—and understand how to navigate your way over and around them—you'll be prepared to meet the challenges and get back to pursuing the work that you love.

Chapter 9

Charting Your Path

There are three kinds of drivers in the world:

- Those who follow maps and directions and feel lost if they don't know what specific series of turns to make (www.mapquest.com was an answer to prayer for these people).
- Those who have never opened the glove box to even look for a map, preferring to find their way entirely on their own reading of the signs, their knowledge of the available roads, and their sense of where they ultimately want to go.
- Those who use maps as a guide but who are also open to exploration, should beautiful scenery, a maze of highway construction, or long-lost relatives lead them—"Let's stop in Spit Junction! I haven't seen Great Aunt Maggie's stepson's niece in twenty years!"

It's the same with careers. There are those who map out every step of their career from the time they sign up for Advanced Placement English in their junior year of high school. There are some who reach the age of forty and still wonder what they want to be when they grow up. Others had a clear-cut plan at the outset—then boredom or market changes or family responsibilities redrew parts of that plan, sending them in a new direction, which they've been able to incorporate into their overall, lifelong career course.

TRUE SUCCESS

One of the hallmarks of a successful career is the ability to maintain upward momentum. Each year we want to earn a little more money, move a little bit higher within our company, add a more significant degree at the end of our name, or gain an increasingly prestigious title.

But maybe this isn't the best way to think of our careers. Or our lives.

Picture your career as a ladder or a series of steps rising higher and higher to Career Heaven, and it's as if you have one—and only one—goal waiting for you at the top. If you're standing halfway up a ladder, you can't easily move it to head in another direction. If you're walking up stairs, those stairs can only lead to one end point. To reach a different destination, you've got to work your way down the steps, search for the right set of stairs that will lead where you want to go, and then start your journey all over again.

Here's the thing: Maybe any image that focuses on moving "higher and higher"—whether ladder, stairs, or a knotted rope—is just plain wrong. In fact, maybe it's exactly the image that will lead to self-doubt and derail our journey toward our real goals.

In the Bible, going "higher and higher" is usually associated with periods of unfaithfulness and human pride, as if humanity keeps trying to move higher on its own, while God just shakes his head in exasperation and shouts at us, "If you know what's good for you, you'll get down from there!"

Take the tower of Babel. We read in Genesis 11:

Now the whole world had one language and a common speech. As men moved eastward, they found a plain in Shinar and settled there....

Then they said, "Come, let us build ourselves a city, with a tower that reaches to the heavens, so that we may make a name for ourselves and not be scattered over the face of the whole earth." (verses 1-2,4)

Seeing where this would lead, God "scattered them from there over all the earth, and they stopped building the city" (verse 8).

Take Satan's temptation of Jesus at the start of Jesus' ministry:

> The devil led him up to a high place and showed him in an instant all the kingdoms of the world. And he said to him, "I will give you all their authority and splendor, for it has been given to me, and I can give it to anyone I want to. So if you worship me, it will all be yours."
>
> Jesus answered, "It is written: 'Worship the Lord your God and serve him only.'"
>
> The devil led him to Jerusalem and had him stand on the highest point of the temple. "If you are the Son of God," he said, "throw yourself down from here…."
>
> When the devil had finished all this tempting, he left him until an opportune time. (Luke 4:5-9,13)

Or take Jesus' brief encounter with a tax collector name Zacchaeus:

> Jesus entered Jericho and was passing through. A man was there by the name of Zacchaeus; he was a chief tax collector and was wealthy. He wanted to see who Jesus was, but being a short man he could not, because of the crowd. So he ran ahead and climbed a sycamore-fig tree to see him, since Jesus was coming that way.
>
> When Jesus reached the spot, he looked up and said to him, "Zacchaeus, come down immediately. I must stay at your house today." So he came down at once and welcomed him gladly. (Luke 19:1-6)

Zacchaeus assumed that climbing higher would actually bring him closer to Jesus. Instead, the tax collector only really met the Lord when he was willing to come down from his perch and go for a walk.

Which brings us to a new image for following the course of our career: the walk. Instead of moving upward on a fairly restricted career ladder, the idea of a walk, a journey, opens up fresh possibilities. We have the freedom to follow a well-worn road or to head off into the bushes and hack out a fresh path of our own. Instead of focusing on "higher and higher," our focus is on "forward and onward." As long as we are moving forward—learning new things, meeting new traveling companions, exploring fresh opportunities, navigating the roadblocks and detours—we are successes.

KEEPING IT FRESH

The German philosopher Arthur Schopenhauer once wrote, "The two foes of human happiness are pain and boredom." I believe boredom is also the biggest threat to your ability to find joy on the job. More than downsizing and demoralizing layoffs, more than interoffice gossip and bad reviews. If you're bored, you'd rather be anywhere else. And that's an awful situation to be in at work.

The good news? Boredom is entirely within our control, and it isn't hard to change. The not-so-good news? Most of us don't even know we're getting bored until it's too late.

You've probably heard the frog-and-hot-water story. (As a former vegetarian and a lifelong animal lover, I'll say, "Please don't try this at home.") The idea is that if you drop a frog into boiling water, the frog will immediately leap

---

In 2001–2002 the job market for chemists was the best in years. In its annual survey, the American Chemical Society found that unemployment had dropped to 1.5 percent from a high of 2.7 percent in 1994.

How much can you earn? The average base salary for full-time chemists was $73,000 in 2002.

---

out. The water is obviously uncomfortable—potentially lethal—and the little amphibian doesn't want anything to do with it. But if you put that same frog in a pan of cold water on the stove, he'll stay there. And he'll continue to stay there as you turn up the heat and gradually increase the temperature. He will adjust to the change, and the rising temperature will lose its shock value. As a result, the little guy is going to end up boiling to death.

Boredom can sneak up on you like that. One day you are challenged by your job and enjoying your work. And then one day you realize you just don't care anymore. It's not that there's no work to do; there's probably more work than ever. But it requires a lot of time in unfruitful meetings or completing paperwork that nobody seems to care about. Without knowing exactly how it came to pass, suddenly you don't feel useful.

No, boredom won't kill you. But it may kill—or seriously wound—your love for your work. It carries a deeper danger as well. If you're bored at work, it's only natural to search for ways to add excitement to other areas of your life. And that hunt for "excitement" can take you down paths that are better not pursued.

The solution? Look for boredom's warning signs and take steps to address them.

Boredom's Warning Signs

Consider the following early-warning signs of boredom. Experience one or two, and you can probably chalk it up to a bad day or a lack of sleep the night before. But if you experience more than a few of these characteristics, that's a sign it's time to take action.

- You no longer look forward to going to work.
- You have ample work on your desk but little or no desire to sit down and do it.
- You notice changes in your nonwork lifestyle; for example, you are spending more money than usual, eating more food than usual or snacking more often, drinking or smoking more.

- You feel increasingly dissatisfied with your current hairstyle, wardrobe, home, car.
- You are spending more time on the Internet or handling personal e-mail at work.
- You check the time frequently, counting the minutes until you can go home.
- You are spending more time talking with coworkers away from your desk.
- You are taking increasingly longer lunch hours and breaks.

"Welcome to Camp Call-a-Lot"

During college I spent my summers as a counselor at a camp for gifted children. For a group of kids who preferred chess to Nintendo, the campers were cute, bright, and surprisingly funny.

I soon learned, however, that their parents were not. After graduation I took a full-time job at the camp's headquarters, manning the phone bank. All day long I fielded calls from parents: "Where is the admissions test held?" "Why didn't my child get accepted?" "I missed the deadline—what are you going to do about it?" Needless to say, the job was considerably less amusing than leading teams of fifth graders in water-balloon wars and egg-toss contests.

I quickly grew tired of the script I had to follow for each call ("Hello, thank you for calling, my name is Abby, how can I help you?") and frustrated with the sheer number of phone buttons in endless combinations (*1 to transfer, #6 to hold, # arrow key plus extension for voice mail).

I had hoped for a career related to children and education. Instead, I found myself running a hotline for overeducated parents pushing their twelve-year-olds onto the fast track to Harvard. I stayed for eight months.

—ABBY GREEN

- You spend more time on personal telephone calls while at work.
- You put off working on projects until the last minute.
- You have begun to occasionally miss deadlines.

Finding Your Boredom Solution

If you're bored in your job, chances are you've lost the momentum that had kept you moving forward. Part of the reason you're bored is because you're standing still. Or worse, you may actually be taking steps backward. So the best response to boredom is to get moving again.

To find out just how and in which direction you should move, ask yourself these questions:

- Do I essentially like the company/organization I'm currently working for?
- Can I expand my current job responsibilities to take better advantage of my gifts and interests?
- Have I discovered a new talent or interest that I'd like to pursue?

The answers to these questions will help you decide whether you can overcome your boredom in your current career or with your current employer, or whether you need to start looking for opportunities elsewhere. Whatever the case, make up your mind to get moving again and leave boredom behind.

CHANGING COURSE

Some people are under the mistaken impression that leaving behind one job or career for something completely different is a sign of failure. Or temporary insanity—as if you'd have to be crazy to give up "everything you've accomplished" to try something new. There might be something to that if your career really were based on a "career ladder," where any move off the one restricted route would put you at risk for some serious bruising. But if you picture your career as a constantly evolving journey along a path of your own choosing… Well, then a new job or a new career is simply an educational trek down a new branch of the road.

One thing's for sure: You won't be alone if you take this approach to your career. According to the Department of Labor, the average thirty-four-year-old has had nine full- or part-time jobs since entering the work force. It's expected that most people will have at least three different careers over the course of their working lives. If you're feeling any hesitation about following your dreams wherever they take you, I hope those facts make the idea of changing course and striking out in a new direction a lot easier to embrace. And I hope the following examples will offer suggestions and information that can make your career journey as smooth and rewarding as possible.

A Change You Can Love

Ellen Kolton woke up one day and realized that she just didn't love her ad agency job anymore. So she started thinking of fresh alternatives. Looking back at her past, she realized that her mother's death due to cancer had given her firsthand insight into the need for health-care professionals who could serve as communication liaisons between patients and hospital staff.

Inspired by the idea of doing such work, Kolton went back to school for a master's degree in public health. She held on to her day job, taking classes at night. It took five years for her to complete her degree this way, but she did it. And she soon nabbed a hospital job as a patient advocate.

Not everyone has to earn a new degree to make a career change.

To find out if your dream is a pipe one or reality, work in the field before you quit your day job. You don't want to make the switch out of frustration, but because it's something you're suited to do.

—JOHN D. RAPOPORT

Susan Galler is another professional who slowly came to feel that something was wrong with her career. As senior vice president of development for a nonprofit organization, she had achieved national recognition for her work. To those who measure success by how high you get on the career ladder, Galler was There. The Top. She had arrived.

But Galler wasn't on a ladder. She was on a lifelong journey toward meaning and fulfillment. Instead of imagining herself at the pinnacle of her career, she saw herself at a crossroads where it was time to make some important choices. She was beginning to hate the fourteen-hour workdays, the endless meetings, the organization's multilayered bureaucracy. "I wanted more creativity, more flexibility, and fewer constraints on how I could use my expertise," she told Anne Hartman, president of Career Investment Strategies, a career and leadership development firm.

With the help of a professional career coach at Hartman's company, Galler was able to pinpoint the things that made her happy both professionally and personally. Her conclusion: She wanted to start a business. As a result, she formed the Galler Group, a consulting firm that helps nonprofits raise money, improve operations, and recruit executives. "I love it," she says.

To make a change for a course that you can love too, consider the following suggestions:

- *Know what you want.* Have a clear picture of what you want to do before trying to convince an employer you can do it. Also, try to pinpoint what you dislike or find unsatisfying or boring about the job you're currently doing, so you don't repeat your choices and find yourself wanting another change six months down the road.

- *You don't have to think Major Change.* Sometimes, changing course is just a matter of switching to a bigger or smaller company, or doing a similar job in a different industry. That may be all you need to get your juices flowing again.

- *Take a "multitrack" approach to your career.* Glance at a map, and you'll see there's almost always more than one way to reach a destination. That applies to your career as well. For example, Track No. 1 might involve doing work that is similar to what you're doing now, but maybe the job responsibilities are balanced differently, or there are additional duties involved that will help you make a shift to another direction. Track No. 2, on the other hand, might be totally different: like going from pro wrestler to wedding photographer. You may have more than one opportunity to get to the kind of work you'll love.

- *Take whatever time you need to take.* If you're spinning your wheels in your current job, you may be eager to move on to something more exciting. That's fine, if you know where you want to go and feel fairly sure about how you'd like to get there. But if you're not quite sure, don't rush your decision. I'm sure that Moses would have loved to have led the Israelites into the Promised Land in a month or two; God saw it differently, and their journey ended up taking forty years. Take the days or weeks that you need to consider your options, focus on your gifts, talents, and priorities, and pray about your decision.

Four Practical Steps

Once you know what change you'd like to make in your career journey, you can begin taking practical steps to get there. Consider these four ways others have made the transition:

1. *Build on your functional skills.* If you like using your core skills and knowledge, consider transferring them to another industry or field you might like more. For example, if you're currently working in the marketing department of a huge, multinational corporation, consider transferring those skills to a small nonprofit organization.

Identify your key talents and skills, then repackage them in a résumé that highlights any volunteer work you may have done in the new field or ways your current job overlaps it. Next, start listing employers to approach, and begin networking with current or past employees at these firms about possible openings.

Building on your skills lets you apply your experience and wisdom immediately and usually results in a smoother transition to a new field.

2. *Start a parallel career.* This strategy lets you keep your full-time job while working weekends or at night in a second profession. Working in a second profession will give you the experience you need to pursue it full time. By keeping your day job, you'll have a steady income while building your credentials.

Make sure that your main employer does not have any rules about employees holding second jobs. (Some do; others are more flexible, assuming your work doesn't suffer.) You can try playing the "Well, I won't tell anyone unless they come right out and ask" game, but that approach might come back to bite you.

Communication skills and thoughtful answers that demonstrate knowledge and experience can quickly overcome [negative] first impressions.

—T. PAUL BULMAHN

---

3. *Make an internal transition.* If you want to stay with your current employer, consider making an internal job change that launches you down a new career path. According to career counselors, this is called "job enrichment." You're seeking new learning opportunities and ways to expand or develop your skills, but you're still looking at staying with your current employer.

Some people don't give a lot of thought to job enrichment, afraid that it just means more work for the same pay. Well, that may be true, at least temporarily. But that's a limited way of looking at your career. Any new skills you can acquire on the job will help you when you're ready to ask for a raise or when you're looking for a new job. They might also help you discover skills and interests you didn't know you had—inspiring you to take your career in a whole new direction.

4. *Just quit.* Say you know what you want to do, and you can't stand being

in your current job one more day. For you, quitting your job outright to do the legwork required to enter a new field *may* be an option. Obviously, this is an approach that you should *not* take lightly. And I'd go so far as to say it shouldn't be taken at all unless you have some money in the bank to keep food on the table and gas in the car during the transition. Unless you have some supportive relatives or a spouse who's willing to "carry" you financially for a while, strive to have at least three to six months' worth of income in the bank before you hand in that resignation.

Perri Capell, senior correspondent for the *Wall Street Journal*–sponsored CareerJournal.com, reported the following story of one professional who did "just quit":

> Julie Jansen, a Stamford, Conn. based career coach and motivational
> speaker, had been a high-level sales and business development executive
> for national outplacement firms for about eight years, rising to the post of
> vice president and New York office manager at her last firm. But although
> she earned a six-figure income, Ms. Jansen says she was "miserable."
>
> She decided to focus on developing a public-speaking career, espe-
> cially after a friend told her that "the only time I would light up was
> when I talked about speaking," she recalls. After doing research about
> this career field for a few months, she quit her job to set up shop as a
> motivational speaker, career coach, and business consultant. "I just cut
> the cord," says the 40-year-old.
>
> To generate work, Ms. Jansen had lunch with everyone she knew
> to tell them of her new venture. Slowly the business grew. "I started my
> business with no business," she says. This strategy works best for execu-
> tives who are highly motivated and confident in their abilities.
>
> "You're forced to act, and it's very exciting," says Ms. Jansen, "but
> the cash-flow situation can be terrifying. I had a lot of stressful
> moments over it." Now she says she earns more than she did at her
> previous employer.

AVOIDING THE BAD CHEESE

We started this chapter mentioning some of the benefits of traveling without maps, of being free to create your own path or branch off onto side trails, of going wherever your skills and passions might lead you. Well, there's a drawback to this approach: You can get lost.

It can happen no matter how much study and planning went into your career choices. It can happen despite your best efforts to follow God's will as well as the leadings of your own conscience. Ten years from now you'll look back and see exactly where you went wrong and how you got off track. But when you're in the middle of it, it just looks like a great situation that has gone totally, inexplicably bad. And fast. Like the new package of shredded mozzarella you just bought that turns out to be moldy the minute you get it home and open it up. According to the date on the package, it's still got three months before it's supposed to lose its freshness. It's as if the finest scientific minds in the country are telling you this cheese should be fine, and yet there it is—the mottled green fuzz.

According to a 2002 survey by Flexible Resource, 59 percent of the respondents were reluctant to approach their bosses about establishing a flexible work schedule.

No one, I hope, would say, "Well, geez, it's still got three months to go before it will *legally* go bad. So I shouldn't worry about using this cheese on my next homemade pizza." (Just tell your roommates you used feta. They'll never know.)

That would be ridiculous. And not so tasty.

But this is exactly the approach we often take when we find ourselves making a career choice that all too soon—and all too obviously—goes bad. It may be that we were meant to wind up in a bad situation; maybe there are great life-lessons we can learn as a result of the experience. Or maybe we were temporarily blinded by the bright lights of a higher salary, the chance to work with people we know and like, the lure of a new city or a more prestigious position. Doesn't matter. If we ignore the fact that we've made a mistake or that we're in the wrong position, it's like telling ourselves that the cheese is fine even as we're brushing the traces of mold from our lips.

I enjoy watching the reality TV show *The Amazing Race.* If you're not a fan yourself, here's the deal in a nutshell: Eleven two-person teams (friends, roommates, spouses, siblings, whatever) compete in an around-the-world race for one million dollars, following clues that take them to their next destination and overcoming "roadblocks" that challenge their on-the-road survival skills. It's a race against time, the other teams, and each other, but the couple to reach the finish line first wins. It's fun to follow all of these teams as they race around the world, putting their relationships, their stamina, their courage, and their travel savvy to the test. Given that all of these people are often driving through strange terrain, guided only by maps and, occasionally, the sometimes haphazard directions of a local resident, it's not too surprising that teams often find themselves going down the wrong road. Of course, it's always hugely frustrating for them. But it's not always detrimental to their standing in the race. They see their mistake, they pull over, they check the map or ask a passerby for help. And they get back in the race. Surprisingly, one season the team that took the most wrong turns ended up being first at the finish line and the winners of the million-dollar prize.

Will we make some wrong choices over the course of our careers? Absolutely. Do those detours mean we'd be much better off sticking to the tried and true? Absolutely not. It may be months or years before you can look back and take stock of everything you've gained along the way. But no matter where your career journey may take you, rest assured that every step along the way can teach you something new and valuable about yourself.

Chapter 10

Making a Difference

Erin Sims graduated from high school in 1998, went to college for two and a half years, decided that wasn't for her, and left to start working full time as a claims adjuster. "I'm a medical-only adjuster for worker's compensation," she says. "That means I pay bills only for employees who are off work for no more than three days. My job is mostly typing, handling bills and records. I work specifically with auto dealers, police and fire departments, city governments. I'm on the phone a lot too, talking mostly with the employers of people who were injured and with attorneys."

She loves the company, and she enjoys her work. But there is one thing she didn't like so much when she began her job, something she still struggles with.

"It's just that I've always been around Christians," she says. "Before this job I worked in an office with three doctors who were all strong Christians. I don't really relate to my coworkers now. They're mostly older ladies, and a lot of them are divorced and don't have families at home. So work is their life. Family stuff is not as important to them, and I'm a real family person. After the first week, I came home crying. It was just horrible.

"I think my coworkers knew from the first day that I was different. I feel like that's a witness right there," Erin says. Even so, she wrestles with the impact she's able to have on her coworkers. "There are three or four girls in my group who've been to church and know about the Bible, but they don't have any desire to go back. I don't see how they can't accept what the Lord did for them," she says. "I just don't understand that."

IN, NOT OF

If you were raised within a caring church community, if you were plugged in to supportive Christian groups in high school and/or college, it may be tough to suddenly find the majority of your waking hours spent among people who don't believe in God or don't believe that Jesus was anything more than a good man or a wise spiritual teacher.

In reaction, you may draw closer to the fellow believers you find at work. There's nothing wrong with this, of course. Befriending other Christians in the workplace is a great way to encourage each other in your jobs and discuss specific challenges you might be facing. But it's going to be tempting to make this group the social focus of your work life. Surrounded by folks who share your own spiritual concerns and values, you may find yourself closing out other, nonbelieving coworkers, creating a comfortable environment where you can feel nurtured and safe.

Companies that create pharmaceuticals are continuing to hire like crazy—from marketing and manufacturing staff to employees in finance, sales, human resources, and research science. Salaries can range from $30,000 to $300,000 a year.

Maybe you've heard the idea that Christians are to be "in" the world, not "of" the world. That is, we're to be an active presence—"salt and light" to use two biblical images—in the world, but we're not to get so caught up with worldly things that we lose our spiritual effectiveness. Knowing where to draw that in/of line can be challenging. It doesn't help that the line will be different for each of us; there's no set of absolute rules that cover every activity, every situation. The call is up to us, our consciences, and the Holy Spirit's leading.

Our tendency, though, is usually to pull back from the world. To set ourselves apart as believers. Do that and you'll certainly keep your faith intact. But you'll be robbing your coworkers of the benefits of your faith. You also may be robbing yourself of relationships with others that could prove personally rewarding.

That's the danger of withdrawing into a "Christian nest" in the workplace. It's warm and it's comfortable, but if we stay there, our non-Christian coworkers will never glimpse the freedom and joy that come with leaving our safe, cloistered world behind and soaring through the sky.

Out of the Nest and into the Mall

A number of years ago, I was stuck in a nest of my own. I had a full-time job at a Christian publishing company. I taught junior-high Sunday school on the weekends. I was single, with free time to spare for movies, getting together with friends, reading, listening to music. Life was great.

So why was I suddenly applying for a second, low-paying, part-time job at the mall?

To be honest, I wasn't sure myself.

But I'd been bothered by a nagging thought: I spent my days going from work to home to church and back again. As a result, I never had any contact with non-Christians. Not unless "Could I get a Big Mac with large fries, please?" counts as contact.

Not that I wasn't happy among the Christians I knew. It was exciting to be surrounded constantly by other believers—people who acted and talked pretty much how I acted and talked, people like me who wanted to know and follow God's will. That kind of environment can nurture and sustain believers.

So yeah, I liked the nest. But I was also yearning to fly. To step out of the "safe" zone and share my beliefs with other people—people who *didn't* act like

I acted or talk like I talked. I wanted to be someplace where I might really make an eternal difference in someone else's life.

So I headed to the mall. There, I applied for a part-time job at a men's gift store where the salespeople were relaxed and friendly (I'm no high-pressure salesman). The owner hired me on the spot. I couldn't wait to meet my coworkers.

The first night Karen, the store's manager, introduced me to my partner for the next four hours. I stared up at a six-foot-three-inch black-bearded bear of a man named Matt. *This is who I'm going to evangelize?* I wondered. It seemed unlikely. *Maybe I'm not really cut out for this,* I told myself. After all, what could Matt and I possibly have in common? What could be the basis for a friendship?

Magic tricks, it turned out. After less than an hour, I learned that when he wasn't at the shop, Matt worked as a professional magician. I was thrilled, having been raised by a minister father who used sleight of hand in some of his sermons. As we talked, I learned that Matt and I had read some of the same books about Houdini, visited the same legendary magic shops in Michigan, New York City, and Chicago, and learned the same ways to make coins vanish and appear again. After one night, I knew conversation wasn't going to be a problem for us.

And it wasn't. Not with Matt, and not with Karen. In fact, conversation came easily with just about all of the other six part-timers. Between helping customers, setting out stock, and dusting the display cases, we talked about family, hobbies, significant others, hopes for the future, and our "real" full-time jobs that paid the bills. If something was important to us, it was bound to come up after a couple of four-hour weeknights or seven-hour Saturdays. So that actually made talk about God fairly commonplace. Everyone knew I worked for a Christian company during the day, so it was only natural to talk about faith and, of course, doubt.

Even so, I was rusty talking about God with people who hadn't been raised in the church and didn't know the lingo. We didn't share the same assumptions about the world. Sometimes we didn't even use the same words in the same ways. But I think that the respect we part-timers had for one another helped us overlook our differences and concentrate on those areas where we agreed. Sometimes that led to late-night talks over nachos at a nearby restaurant. Sometimes it led only to gentle sparring.

"Sparring" kind of sums up my times with Fred, a small, wiry coworker in his midforties with a wild, graying beard, quick eyes, and a raspy laugh. Usually the laughter followed the punch line to a joke that would have earned a rating somewhere between R and NC-17.

"I don't think anybody can prove God even exists," he told me one night, during a lull in business. He seemed to be waiting for my response.

"I can't speak for anyone else," I said, "but I believe what the Bible says about him. And I've seen him working in my own life."

"Does he do tricks for you?" Fred asked, grinning slyly behind his beard. "Like Matt?"

A career change isn't the end of the world; it's possible to honor God in more than one field of work.

—DAVE VEERMAN

I had to laugh. "Trust me. God's more amazing than Matt. And he doesn't use sleight of hand." I began telling Fred about the things I'd seen God do in my life—even the fact that I believed God had put me there to talk to him that night. There were no holy fireworks or anything. Fred didn't change his life because I was some brilliant evangelist. But he did listen. And I took some comfort in the fact that we wouldn't have even been talking about such things unless a part of him—maybe a part he was afraid to admit even existed—was seriously interested in God.

And that just amazed me. I was surprised how willing most of my coworkers were to talk about their spiritual concerns. I had come up with this image of what people in "the world" were like, and it was being contradicted every day by the real-life people I met.

I'd expected outright rejection, yet most of my new friends were not antagonistic to the gospel (although some were disinterested). I'd expected ignorance about Christianity and what it means to be saved, yet most of them knew who Jesus said he was and what he taught. They weren't people I could easily preach at; they were ordinary, interesting people who came to the issue of faith with lots of questions and not a few prejudices and bad experiences. In the end, that only gave us more reason to discuss the Bible and what it really means to live a Christian life.

Making a Difference?

My friends at the shop definitely made an impression on me. But I don't know the extent to which all my talk made any difference in their lives. No one that I know of decided to accept Christ because of my example. Matt was the only person willing to go to church with me.

Still, I feel certain that God used me at that store. Taking that job when I did was the right thing to do. I'm grateful I was there when Matt asked what I thought about him sleeping with one of his girlfriends. When C. J.'s job suddenly changed, and he faced an anxiety-filled cross-country move with his family. After Fred had a bitter argument with his ex-wife. When Gene finally got his pilot's license.

Ultimately, I believe I was able to be Christ's presence for my coworkers, a person who shared their struggles and rejoiced at their successes. Someone who believed sincerely in redemption and salvation and the Resurrection—and who was still willing to take out the trash. (Willing. Not thrilled about it.)

That experience paved the way for the day when my situation changed, and I was spending my workweek, like most believers, trying to live a Christian life among people with an incredibly diverse range of spiritual beliefs.

Living Out Who We Are

My dad used to say, "Christianity isn't a religion. It's a way of life." Witnessing is the same way. In my opinion, it shouldn't be something we *do*. It shouldn't be a pat series of phrases or questions that we slowly work up to in conversation. (The image that comes to mind is of a guy dialing the phone, sweating as he mentally rehearses exactly what he's going to say to the girl on the other end in order to get her to say yes to a date.) Instead, witnessing should be *who we are*. I believe that workplace evangelism is most effective when it's simply us being our everyday Christian selves for the rest of the world to see, day in and day out.

It's the gardener who finishes a day's work on a client's extensive collection of perennials and herbs, steps back, and says, "Wow. God really did an awesome job here, didn't he?"

"Like a Duck on a Pond"

Right after college, having graduated with an English major and no plans, I took a job as a receptionist for a cellular phone company. The building was keycard-protected, which meant that all the other employees were safeguarded in a main office while I sat like a duck on a pond in the lobby. Knowing the cumulative personality of the customer service department, I fully expected to be shot at any moment by a disgruntled cell-phone user.

This job taught me everything I ever needed to know about being a lowly foot soldier in the corporate army. I learned backward logic, busywork, inefficiency, and rudeness as a matter of daily business. I do admit, however, that from being harangued on the phone, I learned to maintain calm under fire and never to take things personally.

—Karin Beuerlein

"God?" the client says. "Looks to me like *you're* the one who put in all the work today."

And that's an open invitation for the gardener to talk about what God's role as Creator really means to him.

It's the chef who sets a casual table in the kitchen for the waitstaff, then leads them in a brief prayer of thanks before they all sit down to enjoy the meal she's prepared.

It's the shop owner who is willing to admit to his employees that business has been down, but he is praying for their future success.

It's the beach lifeguard who hears all of the comments about wanting a good tan and showing off her curves—and who says, "You know, that's not really why I'm here. I think this is exactly where God wants me to be."

It's the delivery guy who knows that his coworkers love heavy metal music, so he loans them a CD of some of his favorite heavy-metal bands— who just happen to be Christian.

It's the nurse, the guidance counselor, the farmer, the part-time playground supervisor, the molecular biologist, the large-animal veterinarian, the circus performer, the PR consultant. It's all believers who strive to do their best work possible, to be themselves—flaws and all—and to reach out with compassion to their coworkers and colleagues.

In Search of the Perfect Role Model

It's weird: The Bible tells us very little about the moneymaking jobs of its main characters. Oh, sure, maybe we know some basics. In the Old Testament we run into a lot of shepherds and farmers and kings and prophets. (How you make a living being a prophet, though, is not really explained.) In the New Testament we learn that Matthew was a tax collector, Luke was a physician, and other early Christians were fishermen or tentmakers. And Jesus, of course, was a carpenter for most of his life. But that's about all we're given—a title or an offhand sentence here and there. Because of the ancient, male-dominated culture of the Middle East, women's "careers" are even less well-represented in

Scripture. (Off the top of my head, I can think of one queen, a fortune teller, and several prostitutes.)

It's not just that the Bible, being a centuries-old book, doesn't offer any practical advice for such modern occupations as optometry or auto mechanics. It's not even all that helpful when it comes to catching fish or mending a good tent. There isn't one word of recorded advice from Jesus—the only perfect human being ever to wield a hammer—on how to craft a table or build scroll shelves out of choice oak. (The directions *were* good when it came to God telling Noah how to build an ark. But how often are you really going to be called on for that?)

Job seekers who can't or who won't promote themselves don't progress. It's as simple as that.

—INTERCRISTO'S *CAREER KIT*

So, okay, the Bible isn't really a good manual for how to insert Tab A into Slot 2B when it comes to work. It doesn't get into those kinds of specifics. And yet it does describe one group of average workers pretty well. It gives us a picture of how they met their manager's expectations or stumbled trying, what their typical workdays looked like, and how they handled triumphs and setbacks. Who are these workers? The disciples—the original Twelve and all of the other believers who came after them.

The Ultimate Job Description

There might be something to be said for the idea that the disciples' "jobs" as disciples were the only ones described in such detail because they represent the work that *all* Christians are called to do. Whether we are gas station attendants, restaurant owners, or airline pilots, we as Christians also are employed as Christ's disciples. In that sense we're all working two jobs (at least!). Maybe the Bible doesn't tell us how to hammer a nail or care for camels because there are other, better ways to learn those jobs. But when it comes to being a disciple, the Bible is the best resource available.

We know from the Gospels and from the letters in the New Testament what a disciple's job description looks like. For now, let's look at six key points. If we are "employed" as disciples, our lives will be marked by our desire to:

1. Serve God.
2. Be a witness.
3. Influence the world.
4. Be used by God.
5. Lead others spiritually.
6. Use our spiritual gifts.

Serve God. The desire to serve God is the best desire we can have. When this is your foundational motivation, the thing that's primarily driving you, God will bless your life and your work:

Whatever you do, work at it with all your heart, as working for the Lord, not for men, since you know that you will receive an inheritance from the Lord as a reward. It is the Lord Christ you are serving. (Colossians 3:23-24)

Be a witness. Consider these verses: "Let your light shine before men, that they may see your good deeds and praise your Father in heaven" (Matthew 5:16); "Make it your ambition to lead a quiet life, to mind your own business and to work with your hands...so that your daily life may win the respect of outsiders" (1 Thessalonians 4:11-12); "Be wise in the way you act toward outsiders; make the most of every opportunity" (Colossians 4:5).

Influence the world. "You are the salt of the earth," Jesus told those who showed up to hear the mountainside sermon recorded in Matthew 5–7. In Jesus' day salt typically served at least two purposes: It was a preservative, and it was a flavoring ingredient for food. Part of our work as disciples is to fulfill those dual purposes in daily life today. We can help to "preserve" a dying world by reflecting the healing, comforting nature of Jesus Christ. We can add flavor to the world by sharing sometimes unpopular opinions, living a lifestyle at odds with some of those around us, and reaching out in love to those whom many in the world have chosen to shun.

Be used by God. Obviously, I have no idea what plans God may have for you. (I don't even know all of the plans God has in mind for me!) But I do know that we'll struggle—finding ourselves on an especially rocky path—if we don't open ourselves up to being used by God, wherever we happen to find ourselves. It isn't difficult. Just ask God to use you at work in whatever way he sees fit. Then pray that you'll have ears open enough to hear his voice and a heart soft enough to follow his leading.

Lead others spiritually. At work it can be tempting to want to rise quickly through the ranks and become a manager everyone looks up to.

As Christian disciples we have a higher calling. God is not impressed with titles, with brass nameplates, or cubicle walls that are six inches higher than everyone else's. (Trust me: I've worked in offices where the "upwardly mobile" actually went around measuring.) No, God is more concerned with the inner person than with the outer symbols of success. For disciples that means "leading in love" rather than "loving to lead."

But maybe "leading others spiritually" seems impossible or inappropriate in a secular workplace. Well, I think that depends on your particular situation. Chances are you aren't going to win any friends—let alone any converts—if you feel compelled to tell your coworkers that they shouldn't go out for drinks after work or that they should dress more modestly in the office or stop flirting with the UPS girl or quit using harsh language in your presence. Besides, I'm not convinced that's what God really wants. (Rhetorical-question alert: If your coworkers actually followed all of those instructions, would they be better people inside? Would their inner lives be transformed?)

The first step is to be a spiritual role model—to model Christlike behavior to the best of your ability as a human being. But I'd suggest that the second step is to be a friend to those around you, someone others will *want* to turn to for advice and help when they're facing hard times at home or wrestling with a moral question or feeling torn apart by an interoffice romance.

Think about it: Jesus did not spend his days seeking out the Pharisees so he could set them straight. Instead, he devoted his days to meeting the people who were needy, tired, and desperate for something that could change their lives for the better. If you have the opportunity to fulfill that role in your own job, consider yourself blessed.

In studies of more than 105,000 employees, a Gallup Organization poll found that "having a best friend at work" was one of the factors most likely to signal a highly productive workplace.

Use our spiritual gifts. We don't know everything there is to know about the lives of the original twelve disciples. But one thing we do know is that they each brought a different set of spiritual gifts to their relationship with Jesus. They weren't twelve generic guys. And their gifts weren't locked in concrete; the disciples changed and developed as they gained experience and understanding.

It's the same with disciples today. Paul's words in the book of Romans are still true:

We have different gifts, according to the grace given us. If a man's gift is…serving, let him serve; if it is teaching, let him teach; if it is encouraging, let him encourage; if it is contributing to the needs of others, let him give generously; if it is leadership, let him govern diligently; if it is showing mercy, let him do it cheerfully. (Romans 12:6-8)

When Worlds Collide

One of the best lessons I've learned from my time spent in the workplace is that Christians come in all varieties. Not everyone believes everything I believe; not everyone acts or talks or thinks the way I've been taught Christians should act and talk and think.

And that's okay. If we think a fellow believer has crossed a moral line—doing something that goes beyond differences in upbringing or opinion and moving into an area of truly sinful behavior—we can talk with him or her about it. We can discuss our personal beliefs and wrestle with how we all live them out in daily life. We can even agree to disagree. And if we end up disagreeing about beliefs we think are absolutely essential—such as the idea that Jesus really was the Son of God, or the understanding that all people are sinners in need of a Savior—there's nothing wrong with stepping back and saying, "You know, I think you're wrong about that," then trusting that, ultimately, the truth lies in God's hands, and he will reveal it, in time, to all of us.

But what if the person we're disagreeing with happens to be our supervisor?

Or what if your boss doesn't have any particular Christian beliefs at all—and she thinks that *your* beliefs are getting in the way of your work? What if you're specifically told to do something that goes against what you believe as a follower of Christ?

Each of us will draw the line in a different place.

Maybe you think it's wrong to be expected to work on Sundays, no matter what kind of impossible deadline is supposed to be met.

Maybe you're a salesperson who has been told to push people toward a particular product or a particular price range, regardless of what they say they want or need.

Maybe you're told to look the other way when certain deals are made.

If you feel constantly compelled to do things you don't agree with as a Christian, it will eventually take its toll. Your faith, your witness, your work, and your own happiness in the job may end up receiving a constant, brutal beating.

Unless you keep watch for such situations, you might find yourself slowly turning into someone you don't want to be. Someone you don't even like.

There is a similar danger if you happen to be working in a job where difficult moral choices are an unavoidable fact of daily life.

If you're a physician, you may have to decide whether to distribute free syringes to illegal drug users to protect them from the spread of HIV. Whether you will offer medical treatment to those without insurance or the funds to pay for your service. Whether you will prescribe birth control for patients under eighteen. What you will tell those who are terminally ill. What you will say to the woman seeking an abortion.

If you're in law enforcement, you may be required to take a human life. You may find yourself in situations where injuring another person is the best solution to a bigger problem. And you may find yourself encountering crime scenes and accident scenes and individuals that make you seriously question whether you're doing what you're supposed to be doing.

If you work in a bookstore, you may be expected to sell books and magazines that you'd rather throw in the trash. If you are an actor, you may be asked to portray people who represent humanity at its worst. If you work in a hotel, you may learn more than you want to know about your neighbors' private lives.

The fact is that no matter what you do, on some days the worlds of your faith and your job will collide. But you can take steps even now that will help you prepare for those collisions and remain secure in your desire to live out a Christian witness in the workplace.

The following ideas can help strengthen your faith and keep your eyes focused on following God—no matter what the workday might bring:

- Start the day with prayer. If you know of something big coming up, ask for the wisdom to handle it. If you're nervous or uncertain about something, seek God's peace. If you can't believe somebody's crazy enough to pay you to do what you love, send a big "Thanks!" God's way.

- Try to do or say one thing every day that shows God's love to someone you meet—coworker, client, or customer.
- As situations come up, ask yourself how you can handle them as a witness for Jesus Christ.
- At the end of the day, thank God for what you have learned, the people you've helped, the job you've accomplished. Ask forgiveness for the places where you fell short. And pray that you can grow into a better person for the days ahead.

THE BEST NEST OF ALL

I started this chapter encouraging you to not be satisfied with a safe, warm "Christian nest" in the workplace, but instead, to stretch outside your comfort zone and really engage your coworkers, Christians and non-Christians alike. But I'd like to end the chapter by highlighting the importance of one Christian nest no believer can afford to be without: a local church.

These days it can be tough to find a church that really meets your needs. For some, "contemporary worship" means "the songs King James sang" back in the day. Other churches wrestle with how to stay relevant in their communities, struggling to meet the needs of an increasingly diverse congregation of different ethnic groups, languages, and religious traditions. Still others get so caught up in righting social wrongs that they put the Bible on a back burner.

Even so, the church continues to be a place where we can share our struggles, unite in our prayers, worship with abandon, and recharge our spiritual batteries. If you are not yet plugged in to a local community of believers, I'd encourage you to make that your number-one priority. Because the faith that we nurture there is what empowers us to make a difference in our working lives.

Chapter 11

Creating Great Music

In my dream it was early morning. The air was cool and clear, and I was leaving the house for work or school. (It's sometimes not clear where you're going in a dream.) I hopped on my bike, had to kind of hang off one side to balance myself (again, blame the dream), and took off down the street.

It wasn't my real, current street, but a street from my past, rearranged and improved thanks to dream-logic. I flew down a small hill, followed by a slightly bigger drop that took me past very neat, new red-brick buildings. I squeezed the hand brakes to stop at the first corner. It looked like a successful, clean, solid middle-class neighborhood. Normal.

Except for that guy on the corner waving a baton.

I thought maybe he was directing a marching band that was coming down the street from the other direction. But no. There was no music anywhere that I could hear. Just this one guy. Waving his baton like he was conducting an orchestra.

Then I looked farther down the street and saw that he was not alone. In the next block, there were more people with batons. Some were walking down the sidewalk, others were milling about in the middle of the street—*I'll have to pedal around them,* I thought—but they were all lost in their own private concerts, conducting music that I couldn't hear, but enjoying it immensely. They all looked absolutely content.

I woke up thinking that these dream images actually have something to say about how we approach our careers.

When you find yourself doing work that relies on your God-given gifts and talents and feeds into your personal passions, work can be bliss. That doesn't mean there won't be hurdles to face or that you'll never stumble home with a splitting headache or a choice word for your coworkers or your employees or your supervisor. But those days will be the exceptions. And you'll be able to weather them because you'll know—you'll *know*—that you are doing exactly what you should be doing, and you're loving it.

Hopefully this book has helped you lay the foundation for that kind of career, a foundation you can build on over the entire course of your working life. But there's only so much that written resources and other people can do for you. You are the conductor of the band that only you will truly be able to hear. You'll be the first one to notice any undesirable dissonance, any out-of-tune or missing instruments. You are the one who will decide when to move on to the next part of the song, when to repeat something familiar or explore something brand new, when to rock out and when to quiet down.

In that sense, the sound of your career is up to you. But there are certain ways you can go about achieving that sound—shaping your career and your life—that will help guarantee your success.

CREATING YOUR SONG

Between my first and second years in college, I had the opportunity to travel with a school-sponsored singing group. Seven of us were chosen by the school to travel to churches throughout the Midwest and East, meet with the local youth groups, do concerts, and also promote the college and its music program. It was my summer job that year—as I recall, the school paid each of us fifteen hundred dollars toward the next semester's bill—and it was one of the greatest times of my life.

One of the best things, though, was that we got to record an album. (Back in the days when albums were black and played by a needle.) Except for a few promotional films that had been released by European bands (ABBA and Queen are the only ones I can remember seeing), this was before the age of real music videos. And it was definitely before VH1's *Behind the Music.* So the workings of recording studios were still pretty mysterious. Until we stepped into that studio in suburban Chicago, I had no idea how groups recorded their songs.

It was an amazing experience. And despite a lot of advances in recording technology since then, the work is still done basically the same way today.

Here's how it works. Unless a band is recording something "live"—that is, playing and singing together as if they were actually performing a concert— the majority of the instruments and vocals are recorded separately on individual tracks over a period of days, weeks, or months. By recording every sound on a separate track, the engineers can adjust each individual element over the course of a song, allowing for fine-tuning of the mix and perfect or near-perfect performances. (If the drummer screws up, he just keeps recording his part or even just the problematic couple of beats until he gets it right. Chances are, his bandmates aren't even in the studio with him.)

The trouble with unemployment is that the minute you wake up in the morning you're on the job.

—SLAPPY WHITE

Most recording artists build up their songs from a rhythm track—drums, congas, percussion, synthesized rhythms, whatever. Think of it as the musical skeleton of the song. And to keep the rhythm instruments perfectly synchronized, the performers will often rely on what's called a "click track," which is like having a metronome constantly playing in your headphones while you're playing your part. The click track establishes the tempo and helps make sure the rhythm people stick to it. (The click track, by the way, never ends up being heard in the finished recording.)

Once the drums and percussion tracks are laid down, then a group might add several rhythm guitar and keyboard tracks. At some point a lead guitar will come in, along with the backing vocals. Usually, the lead vocal will be the last addition to the mix.

And that's pretty much it. The rest of the aural mix will largely end up being the responsibility of the recording engineers and the producers; they'll decide exactly how each individual song gets pulled together from all of these separate tracks. Like expert chefs, they'll take all of the ingredients, mix them together in what they believe to be the right proportions, and end up with songs that, with any luck, people will actually want to pay money to hear. It will most likely be the best they can produce given the musicians' abilities, their own technical expertise and interest in the project, the time available, and of course, the budget.

Believe it or not, recording a song is a lot like building a career you will love.

God Is My Click Track

I've played drums for most of my life. But I'll be the first to admit that it's a struggle to maintain a solid, unwavering tempo. If I get caught up in a song, I'll notice myself gradually speeding things up. And if I don't quite remember how I played a song the last time, it's not unusual for me to start out too slow or too fast and have to make adjustments along the way.

A lot of us face similar challenges in our lives and our jobs. We need a steady, unwavering beat that keeps us on track, that keeps us from rushing ahead on our own into places we don't belong, that keeps us from getting mired in difficulties or overwhelmed by our circumstances.

For me and for many others, God is that unwavering beat. He is the driving force that can keep us progressing at the right tempo, leading us ahead through Scripture, through prayer, and through the counsel of other believers. In careers where change is almost a daily fact of life, God fills a unique, steadying role: He remains the same yesterday, today, and tomorrow. And when we lose our way, he is constantly there to bring us back on track.

There will be times when we'll shut him out. We'll feel secure in our own ability to keep things going at the right speed, for the right length of time. We may even do fine for a while. But I think we'll eventually pay the price for turning down the volume on God's voice. It's hard to keep all of the many elements of our lives straight when we lose our hold on the solid, guiding truth of God's love for us.

Public schools in the United States expect to need 2.4 million new teachers by 2012.

Don't wait for something to go wrong before you step back and take stock of God's role in your career. Make a point of regularly asking yourself:

- Am I still listening for God's guiding voice?
- Am I trying to follow God's tempo?
- Are all of my choices in line with his beat, or do some of them sound out of place?
- What steps do I need to take to get back on track?

We Got the Beat!

It's impossible to imagine a sporting event nowadays that isn't accompanied by the *THUMP-THUMP CLAP* rhythm of Queen's "We Will Rock You." (Correction: I don't think anyone does it at golf tournaments. Or polo. But just about every other sporting event does it.) Being a Queen fan, I love it. Even without a single lyric of the song, that rhythm is enough to get the blood pumping and send out a clear message: "*We* have what it takes to be champions!"

In creating the song of your career (I'll assume that phrase doesn't sound too stupid to you), think of confidence and attitude as your drums and percussion.

Pro drummers can't be tentative. If they're not pounding their instrument, all of those electric guitarists who've blown out their eardrums won't be able to hear the beat and follow along. A jazz musician might "play" his drums, but a rock drummer has to beat 'em. And when it comes to making music in your career, you definitely want to rock. That means exuding confidence. Having an attitude that shows you believe in yourself and what you're doing in life.

As Christians, we must seek to understand how we fit into God's plan to transform the world.

—TOM SINE

To be honest, I still struggle with this point. When I meet people—new people and old friends alike—my tendency is to downplay what I do for a living. "What are you working on?" they'll ask. And I'll actually shrug and say, "Oh, nothing," when, in fact, I might be writing a book and working on a couple of magazine articles. I might have recently updated my Web site or applied for a fellowship. I may have just been appointed to a committee in a writers association. But still I say, "Oh, nothing." Why? I'm not sure.

Maybe I'm afraid it sounds like bragging to talk about writing a book, even though writing books is a basic part of how I earn a living. (Can you imagine a mechanic being ashamed to say, "Well, today I replaced a set of brakes"? Uh…no.)

It could be that my last writing session wasn't particularly productive, so I don't feel all that successful at the moment. Or maybe I pitched an idea to a magazine I really wanted to break into, and the magazine said, "No, thanks." Or a freelance check I was counting on still hadn't shown up in the mail. Then again, maybe I'm just shy.

Who knows.

The result is that I end up not sounding confident. Which means I also don't sound successful, like someone it would be good to know and work with. And if I don't believe enough in myself to talk proudly about my accomplishments and current projects, how can I expect anyone else to jump on my bandwagon?

There is another reason to cloak yourself in an attitude of confidence and talk about your work: The more others know about what you do or what you're *wanting* to do, the more they will be able to help you. If you just closed a big deal, let people know. They may know other individuals who would make good customers for your company. If you're thinking about "moving up and moving on," let some of your friends know; they may be able to connect you with the perfect position elsewhere.

As you navigate your career, ask yourself:

- Am I beating my own drum? Or am I tentative about my career and my accomplishments when I'm around others?
- Am I someone whose confidence draws and inspires others?
- Am I proud of the work I'm doing? If not, what needs to change?

Layers of Support

In a rock band, it's rhythm guitars and keyboards. For rap artists, it's often razor-sharp synthesizers. For pop stars it might be thick layers of keyboards, guitars, digitized sounds, and a tight group of background singers. No matter what form it takes, it's musical support. A "wall of sound" as it was called in the glory days of Motown (think The Supremes). It enhances the basic beat and undergirds the melody.

In terms of careers, "support" involves a variety of things.

Education. Learning doesn't stop with a diploma or a degree; it's something you'll be doing the rest of your life. You can find a lot of useful information in trade magazines and seminars. But you may need more formal training or additional schooling to really thrive at what you're doing now. Or maybe you're wanting to change course and explore something new; you'll need educational support to succeed at what you want to do next.

Finances. Obviously, you need to earn enough money to support yourself. But it's easy to overlook all of the other financial blanks that should be filled in too.

For instance, if you are a Christian, you should be tithing appropriately to your local church or to a Christian ministry you trust and believe in. "Tithing" means giving 10 percent of what you earn to God's work. If you're just starting out, giving up 10 percent may sound impossible. If that's your situation,

---

"Desperately Seeking Employment"

I worked part time taking personal ads.

I started out on the phones, helping callers list their qualities (or those they wished they had) and those they sought in a mate. I learned to correctly punctuate strings of abbreviations ("DWM, 45, seeks H/W/BF, under 40, for LTR"). I became quick to suggest acceptable physical descriptions (slim, Rubenesque) and to reword those that were not (buxom, chesty). I hung up on heavy breathers.

Eventually I voiced my interest in doing more "editorial" work. A few months later I won my first full-time job proofreading the finished personal-ad sections before they shipped to newspapers nationwide.

In the production department I quickly learned how to use proofreading marks, comment on layouts in the language of graphic design, and survive the pressure of daily deadlines. I also gained experience using graphic design programs, which has been a strong selling point in job interviews.

—GENEVIEVE C. RAJEWSKI

you have a choice: Make 10 percent your minimum goal to shoot for—and give as much as you possibly can in the meantime—or go ahead and start tithing now, trusting that God will honor your faithfulness and provide for your needs. (Not to weigh you down with guilt or minimize your very real financial concerns, but personally I don't think *not* tithing is a real option for committed believers. But that's between you and God.)

Money concerns don't stop there. Are you saving for the future—perhaps contributing to a retirement account at work or socking away some extra cash in a money market account, just in case you find yourself out of work for a while at some point?

Are you working to either avoid debt or pull yourself out of debt (say, thanks to the helpful folks at Visa and MasterCard)? The less debt you have, and the more cash and invested money you have, the freer you are to provide for yourself—and maybe a family—and to support important causes.

People. When we think of a "support network," most of us probably think of our immediate family and our closest friends. The people we can turn to if disaster strikes; the people we can whine to. But in a career sense, support can be a whole lot broader.

Seek out mentors— older, wiser, and more experienced professionals who can offer you sound advice, job leads, encouragement, and if you need it, a whack on the side of your head if you're heading toward a potentially stupid career decision. (A hard smack may not sound so appealing, but it can do wonders for your career growth.)

Also, look for opportunities to be a mentor for someone else. That act of giving may go against what you think "support" should be. Think again. The more you're willing to give to others, the more your own career—and life— will be enriched.

Develop a network of colleagues (at your own company and others) to whom you can turn for industry information, leads, career advice.

Church. "Church" means more than just the people involved there. It takes relationships with others and combines them with our own relationship with God. Are you plugged in to a supportive group of believers? Is your church helping you grow as a Christian?

When it comes to support in general, ask yourself:

- Do I have the knowledge I need to succeed in my current position? Do I have what I need to get to the next level in my career?
- What part of the financial picture do I need to work on most? Have I established financial priorities that accurately reflect my spiritual and personal beliefs?
- Am I seeking out—and providing—the kind of people-focused support that needs to take place?
- Am I as involved as I should be in a local group of believers?

Taking the Lead

On my music shelf The Corrs and The Cranberries sit next to Creed. Sarah McLachlan shares shelf space with Alanis Morissette, No Doubt, Stacie Orrico, Plumb, and Prince. Rebecca St. James is sandwiched in by Todd Rundgren, Shakira, Squirrel Nut Zippers, and Shania Twain.

Obviously, I like a lot of different kinds of music. One of the constants, though, is the quality and personality of the lead vocalists. For me, "quality" goes beyond the question "Can they actually sing?" I like voices that are distinctive in some way, voices that I could immediately identify if someone were to put on a random CD and hit Play. Voices that have a unique and expressive style.

Personality comes through in the kinds of songs the singers sing. I tend to be drawn to songs with lyrics that are meaningful or fun or interesting or important. And I don't always have to like what I first hear; in fact, I enjoy music that takes endless playing to figure out and fully appreciate. The first time I heard Alanis Morissette, I wasn't so sure she could actually sing. And I found her lyrics occasionally too strong and embarrassingly personal. But the more I've listened to her, the more I've been convinced that, yes, she can actually sing. And although her words are sometimes hit-you-between-the-eyes blunt, she's exploring deep issues about relationships and family that are either glossed over and prettied up in other pop songs—or they're never mentioned at all. I've come to appreciate Morissette's courage and the integrity of her message, even though I still sometimes cringe at the way that message is delivered.

As an accompanist I've played the piano for a lot of amateur singers who try hard to sound like the artist who originally recorded their song. I've also accompanied singers who needed to develop the enthusiasm and personality needed to "sell" a song to an audience; they sang too softly or didn't make eye contact with their listeners, or they didn't keep up with the beat or couldn't quite stay on pitch. Their hearts were definitely in the right place. But for whatever reason, the quality and the personality weren't there to back it up.

According to the *New York Times Magazine*, personality testing in the workplace is now a $400-million-a-year industry.

In terms of your career, you are the lead singer. You shape your career like a singer shapes a song. Not everything is riding on you, of course. You've got a solid support team surrounding you. And you're being ultimately led by God's steady beat. But confidence and attitude are up to you. And so is the final performance, where you're out on the front lines actually *living* this career, day in and day out.

That can be scary. It can also be a lot of fun. You can make your career whatever you want it to be. You've got the support you need; step out in faith. You can turn a boring job into a challenging, rewarding job. You can go places and do things that you didn't think were within the realm of possibility. You can learn things about yourself and the world around you that are unexpected and exciting. You might even discover that you have the resources to handle adversity, to bounce back from work experiences that you thought would make you crumble. You can succeed. Even better, you can thrive. And have a terrific time doing it.

Final Words

People tell me I'm lucky to be doing what I'm doing for a living. Maybe. But it's amazing how "lucky" people can be when they set their sights on a dream and go after it. The universe smiles on us in ways it can be hard to imagine until you've experienced it.

And that's my final prayer for you: that you would experience the incredible satisfaction that comes from finding *your* perfect job and doing what you love for the rest of your life. That the question, "So, what are you going to do *now?*" would fill you with excitement about the possibilities in store for your future. That you would enjoy the journey as much as the destination. And that you would do everything in your power to share with those around you the joy you've found along the way.

Real Stories from Along the Way

When you're heading into uncharted territory it can help to know that others have experienced similar hills and valleys and encountered some of the same wild animals.

The people I talked to as I wrote this book offered me a window into a variety of individual gifts, worldviews, opinions, and decisions; I wanted to include some of their stories here, in their own voices. As you wonder just how far you can go in the world, as you seek out exciting careers that capitalize on your own skills, passions, and abilities, I hope the following views from the front lines will offer encouragement, inspiration, and some very practical advice for finding your way while staying true to who God created you to be.

JOHN WELCH
Letter Carrier

I was working as a government office clerk and was running the office mail down to the post office. I started talking to the people who worked there. I asked what they made and found out it was substantially more than I was earning.

I didn't apply right away, because you have to have a near-perfect driving record, and I didn't. So I waited until that cleared up and then I arranged to take the test the post office requires. Before then, though, I took a class on how to take the test. It was the best thirty-five dollars I ever spent!

The test covers memory, proofreading skills, your ability to follow instructions, put numbers in sequence, that kind of thing. Those things are important, because you might get placed on a different route each day, and you need to be able to work accurately and efficiently.

I arrive at work at seven in the morning and swipe a badge to get on the clock. Then I go to what's called a "turnback" area, where clerks have put the letters and flats—newspapers, shoppers—for my route. I spend about two to three hours getting mail ready for the street, putting all of the letters into slots that match my delivery pattern. Then I pull everything down from my case and band everything together. (I take out between eighteen and twenty feet of mail a day.) Organization is one of the keys to the job.

My leaving time is 10:40. I get gas if I need it and then go to the mail route.

We use electronic scanners so the post office can track our time for the day. There's a bar-code sticker placed in the first mailbox on the route, at the last house I go to before I break for lunch, at the first house *after* lunch, and at the last house at the end of my route. It makes for a structured day. If you're on a route you're unfamiliar with, you can use the bar codes to judge your speed. But if there is inclement weather or lots of Express Mail, that adds time to your day.

We're on a base salary, but we have the opportunity to earn overtime. I just have a high-school diploma, but for the last fifteen years I've made over fifty thousand dollars a year working at the post office. We have a good retirement plan, insurance, good base pay, and you're outside every day. There are many benefits.

The downsides? Well, thirty-five degrees and rain! Dogs attacking you. A very "interesting" work schedule, where you have Sundays and then one rotating day off. When you're a rookie, you work holidays—Christmas, New Year's—and Sundays. Also, in order to be in management, you only have to have worked at the post office for six months. So it's possible for someone who has never carried mail—maybe they've just sold stamps at the office window—to get into a position where they're telling someone who's done it for twenty years how to do it faster and more efficiently.

My faith played a significant part in my job after the terrorist attacks on September 11, 2001, and the anthrax scare that came after. Two postal workers who died from anthrax-contaminated mail lived ten miles from our house. I was on vacation when the attacks happened, and when I came back everyone was wearing rubber gloves. But there was a warning on the glove box that said they could not protect you from biohazards. Everyone wore them anyway. I dealt with the threats and anxiety through prayer. There was just no other way. In the flow of the mail, an anthrax-contaminated letter could rub up against your letter, and you'd never know it.

I think being a mailman is the best job in the world. I love it. I'm truly a people person, and I have the gift of gab. What I love best about the job is the people-to-people contact. I've been in this neighborhood since 1990, and I'm part of the community, even though I don't live there. Where I deliver, the kids walk to school in the morning, and they all say hi to John the mailman. When a block has a block party, they invite John the mailman.

GLYNDA RICE
High-School Math Teacher and Volleyball Coach

I teach high-school mathematics, coach volleyball, and am a Young Life leader. We have about sixteen hundred students at the high school. It's in suburban Columbus, just north of town. Some would consider it ritzy, but we have students from all academic and economic backgrounds and abilities. I've been teaching fifteen years, the last ten at this high school.

My degree was in psychology, and I did a career program in youth ministry. After I graduated I traveled with Sports Ambassadors' basketball team in South America. Then I went back to Ohio and into youth ministry, starting a program of after-school sports in elementary schools.

When the support money ran out, I worked as an adolescent counselor for a year. I worked with kids who were fourteen to eighteen, who either just wanted someone to listen to them or who were there because they had been expelled or suspended from school or had been sent there by the courts. When they were meeting with me, all of my clients would want to make these big changes in their lives. Then they'd go back to school, meet up with their old friends who expected them to act a certain way, and they'd go back to their old ways. After watching that happen, I eventually decided that high school really had the most influence on these kids' lives. So that's where I wanted to be.

When I thought about teaching, I focused on science and math. I would have had ethical problems with teaching science, though (evolution, for example), so I decided to teach math. I went back to college for two and a half years to get certified to teach.

Now at that point, it had been ten years since I had had math in college—and I didn't really like it! And even now it's not like I sit at home and do math problems all the time. But I don't hate it now. And when students tell me that they don't like math, I can relate. I can say, "I didn't either." And when they say that they just don't get something, I can honestly say, "I used to have a hard time with that too."

Teaching requires a lot of time. People think you just show up at eight o'clock and leave at two o'clock, but I could easily do four hours of work a day outside the classroom—grading, keeping records, that kind of thing.

I've never just been a teacher, though. I'm also a coach and a Young Life leader. Teaching pays the bills and gets me around the students, but leading Young Life is my platform for sharing my faith. And coaching is my gift.

As a Christian in the public school system, a lot of students know what I stand for. They know I'm a caring teacher. And when it comes to sharing your faith, there are a lot of things you *can* do in the public school system. I think it says something to high-school students when I teach them all day, spend time coaching them after school, lead them in Young Life Club, and am still willing to go to McDonald's afterwards and listen to their life stories. For these kids, it's all about relationships. That's why I'm there: to be kind of like "God with skin on."

Advice: I'm already on my third career, so I'd have to say there's nothing wrong with changing your mind as you go through life! Keep a broad focus to find out what your gifts are.

ERIC WOOLBRIGHT, DDS
Oral Surgeon

My specialty is called oral and maxillofacial surgery. It's a specialty of dentistry that has wavered back and forth between medicine and dentistry. I would categorize us as jaw surgeons.

The most common thing that we're known for is the removal of embedded or impacted wisdom teeth; most general dentists do not remove wisdom teeth or third molars. The other areas of surgery that we do include reconstructive surgery—due to accidents, injury, tumor, gunshot wounds, or car accidents—where pieces of the jaw are missing. We can rebuild portions of the jaw and teeth and gums, grafting a bone from various places in the body, grafting soft tissue that resembles gum, rebuilding teeth with dental implants.

Another broad category we specialize in is called pathology, removing cysts and tumors that are either benign or malignant and doing biopsies of the mouth and surrounding structures. Under pathology is TMJ surgery. On some people, the jaw joint has a cartilage that gets damaged—kind of like an arthritic condition—so we repair that.

Another category is orthognathic surgery, essentially for people who come to us from an orthodontist. They went thinking they had crooked teeth, but it turns out to be a mismatch in their jaw, where the upper jaw is way too large or their face is way too long. In conjunction with an orthodontist who straightens teeth, we can make cuts in the jaw and reposition it.

The other large area is trauma, basically fixing broken jaws and surrounding broken bones. Tomorrow I'm taking care of a young lady who, two years ago, was in an automobile accident. We've had to fix her two broken jaws, and she lost twelve teeth, six upper and six lower. She's been in a long-term rehab setting due to long-term neurological damage.

There was never a beam of light that came on and told me to do this. I went to college to be an accountant. After one semester I realized I wasn't good with numbers. So I defaulted to the biological sciences because they were basically about memorization: You read something and you regurgitate it. I knew

I could do that; my mind was geared toward memorization. So I began a zoology degree. With that, you're pretty much looking at getting a Ph.D. or teaching. I'd always had a vague interest in the medical side, having an uncle who was a general physician. I knew I didn't want to do that because I saw the absolute dominance that had on his life, being called out at all hours. But I had some interest. Then I saw a TV special on a guy who was repairing clefts in the palate. I thought maybe I should investigate that.

So I looked at who fixes cleft, and I found out either plastic surgeons or oral max surgeons do it. Oral surgery looked more appealing to me. You have to go to dental school first, so I figured that even if I didn't make it all the way to oral max, I'd at least be a dentist.

After I got my B.A. in biology, I went to dental school. I wasn't really gung-ho about it. I essentially said, "God, if this is what you want me to do, you'll give me one of the residencies I've applied for. I'm only going to try once." I applied to three in Chicago. I was one of more than three hundred applicants going for only three positions. I got accepted into the program at Cook County Hospital.

Once you get past the second year of dental school, the whole thing tends to be like a job. The last two years of dental school, you're seeing patients. If you enjoy doing dentistry, you'll be doing what you like to do. In a residency you're paid something like twenty thousand dollars a year; it is school, but you're doing what you want to do. You're learning, but it's hands-on learning and interactive. For me, the years went by very rapidly.

It really worked out well—even for not going in with a lot of enthusiasm. As I talk with other colleagues, they've been gung-ho from the beginning, thought they'd be a failure if they didn't make it. For me, things just kind of fell into place. I thoroughly enjoy what I do. I love the medicines and pharmacology of it. The only downside about it is the bureaucracy, the paperwork, and dealing with insurance.

Most oral surgeons during a five-day workweek would probably spend four of those days on office-based surgery: wisdom teeth, replacing dental implants, minor biopsies. One day a week is when we typically try to schedule our more major hospital surgeries. But broken jaws happen at all hours. Most people who are violent like to do that stuff at two or three in the morning.

By and large, most oral surgeons are in towns of at least thirty to forty thousand people and then have a perimeter around that to draw from. I think you'd have great difficulty sustaining a busy practice if you're in a smaller town. Springfield, Illinois—where I live—is a town of more than one hundred thousand people, and we draw from about an hour away. There are only six oral surgeons in Springfield, and two of them are semiretired.

The salary range for a full-time private-practice practitioner would be somewhere between $250,000 and $500,000 a year. Being a professor at a dental school pays somewhere between $60,000 and $80,000 a year. (Because the pay for academic positions is so much less than going into private practice, there are currently about fifty unfilled academic positions across the country.)

In terms of day-to-day practice, I have, over the years, been able to make my work part of my worship and faith. There are a lot of organizations to help you do that. I've connected with a Christian medical and dental society, which offers programs on how to share your faith when appropriate, making your work your worship. I always pray before procedures. Sometimes I feel led to pray out loud with patients, sometimes not. I also try to have my spiritual antennae up. There have been some opportunities to reach out, particularly when we see sixteen-year-old kids who drink a lot and drive their cars into telephone poles. They survive, but they smash up their faces. After traumatic events like that, a lot of people are searching for what they want to do; life's a big question mark to them. When I go to see them in the hospital, they may be asking spiritually significant questions. Sometimes that'll prompt me to share certain aspects of faith with them. And with oral cancer, people ask "Why?" and "Why me?" I pray for my patients.

Advice: First of all, to do this job you have to really be a people person, because you're constantly dealing with people. You have to be able to build a good team and not be a solo act; for instance, I have three nurses, and there are four surgeons in my practice. But you also have to be able to deal with the ups and downs of people facing surgery. They all have different concerns. They might not want to face their diagnosis or what's going to happen.

You also have to enjoy the basic biological sciences and be able to memorize a lot of data and regurgitate it. Oral surgery involves motor skills, too. You have to enjoy doing things with your hands.

Finally, I'd say research your job a little better than I did. One of the things that got me interested was the surgeon on TV repairing clefts. What I found out, though, is that cleft patients are extremely rare in the United States.

TARA GREENWAY
Actress and Playwright

I've earned more money word processing than I ever did acting. I've worked with inner-city teenagers, and I've temped in law offices. I'm also licensed as an interfaith minister.

But what I *am* is an actress.

For me, a typical day starts with waking up and complaining about the lack of roles! Just kidding. When I first started out, I went to every possible audition—three or four a week for three years or so. And about twice a year, I'd get the part. That's fairly typical. So you have to deal with a lot of rejection.

You buy *Backstage*—a paper with articles on the theater and all the audition listings for theater, student and independent films, etc.—circle what you feel qualified for, go to open calls, send in your head shot, send out pictures, résumés, cover letters. I might call my agent, but I certainly don't call my agent every day.

I belong to a theater company that gets together every Monday night, and we support each other. It helps to have an artistic home, someplace where you can get support and good feedback.

My husband is also an actor. We understand that this is a passion and this is who we are. Neither one of us is going to say, "Why don't you just give up on this and get a desk job?"

When I looked at colleges, I knew I wanted to go to a Christian college with a theater program. I got a lot of stage experience, and it was fun and built my confidence. But it didn't prepare me to be an actress in New York City. So many of the people here know each other from school—Yale, Juilliard, and NYU. Acting is like anything else: If you're hiring someone, and there are eighty strangers and one person you know—and the person you know can do a good job—you're going to pick the person you know.

So you don't have a lot of power as an actor. That's why I started writing. I wrote and performed a one-woman, off-Broadway show (in collaboration with Ariane Brandt) called *Missionary Position,* and I'm now about two-thirds of the way through writing another play.

At first, my Christian faith was a real deterrent to my work as an actress. Christians are taught that we shouldn't be angry, we shouldn't be sexy. But people don't write dramas about getting up in the morning and doing the dishes. I've had to learn how to be totally open about my emotions as an actress and not hide anything or hold anything back. There's nothing I wouldn't audition for because of my faith.

Advice: If you want to work in the theater, be true to yourself. Do it for the work, the art. Don't do it to get approval from reviewers or directors or publishers. And don't allow others to be the judge of your success.

NATHAN POTRATZ
General Manager, Gordon Chevrolet, Inc.

After majoring in religion and philosophy in college, I went to seminary for a year in Sioux Falls, South Dakota, the same school my dad had gone to. So I moved out to South Dakota and ran into a friend of mine. He was pastoring a couple of churches outside of Sioux Falls, but he was going to graduate, so he suggested I take his place. These two churches shared a seminary student as a pastor and then split the cost. I thought it was a good opportunity that I could do for three years. It paid $160 a week, which I could supplement by working at a camera store, which I had done before.

So on Sundays my wife, Tracey, and I would get up at the crack of dawn and drive fifty miles to the first church. After one morning service we drove to the second church for the second morning service. We spent the day with a church family then returned to the first church for the evening service. It was an experience, especially when it began to snow. We did that for three months. Tracey would play piano and sing solos. It was like the Nate and Tracey Show, two times in a row. For me, it was just a hardship to come up with what to talk about every week. I really wasn't prepared for doing that.

I was miserable and had some long conversations with Tracey about it. I thought maybe I wasn't really called to be in the pastorate, that maybe I had felt like I was trying to follow in my father's footsteps. I called my dad, and he said, "You've got to do what you think is right." So I resigned from the churches, one of which had just decided to call me as their pastor for the next three years! They were stunned, but I felt it was the right thing to do. I finished out the year at school, doing the work for a one-year biblical studies certificate.

I had a friend at the seminary who was selling Chryslers part time while he was going to school. So I asked him what it was like to sell cars. The secret, he said, was to "Dress nice and call people back. If you do that, you'll be successful, because most people don't do that." He went on to tell me, "I sell Chryslers part time and I'm making fifty thousand dollars a year doing it—and I'm doing it in Sioux Falls, South Dakota!" We were broke and didn't really have a place to go, so we moved close to family near Detroit, and I started knocking on doors to find a job.

Eventually I went to Stuart Chevrolet and had an interview. Very few people come in looking for car positions with a suit and tie and a résumé, so I got hired right away. I moved from car sales into sales management, then moved into the finance department at another dealership in Michigan, then I filled an opening at the first store for a general manager and worked there for a few years. Then the owner called me and asked if I was willing to relocate.

"Would you move to Florida?"

I'd never even dreamed of moving, I told him.

"Well, you've got five minutes," he said.

I called Tracey and asked if she wanted to move to Florida, even though we'd been in our new house just three months. She said, "I guess so." Two weeks later, I got on a plane and headed to Florida to manage a dealership. I think I'm where God wants me now. I've seen how the hand of God has worked in my life over the years. I don't have any regrets about any of the moves I've made.

I often liken my job to two jobs combined: a kindergarten teacher and the guy who cleans up after the horses in the parade. I'm either babysitting or cleaning up mistakes. I'm supposed to be a visionary—direct the advertising, look for new ways to do business, make sure we're following procedures and following the law, have the right people in the right jobs, and have accountability for all of the money. But usually I'm dealing with customers who've gone through all of the managers under me and still haven't been satisfied. Usually it's the customers asking for something they don't have coming. I get the extreme cases; the managers handle the rest.

I control all of the advertising, which takes about five or six hours a week. I oversee the display, the technicians. We have about eighty-five full-time employees and twenty to twenty-five part-time employees. Fourteen managers work under me. Salary-wise, a general manager can earn from $200,000 to $300,000 a year. Normally, general managers are paid some type of salary— $40,000 to $50,000—and then they get a percentage off the bottom-line profit of the store, anywhere from 5 to 15 percent. So they're paid similar to the owner and have the same concerns.

The bad reputation that car salesmen have doesn't concern me. Personally, I run across it even in my own family. Tracey's relatives scoffed at the idea of selling cars when I first started, but it's a very lucrative business. And you can bring honesty and integrity to the table. Sure, you can lie to make more money, but in the end it will come back to haunt you. When we hire people, that's the first thing we tell them: Don't ever lie to a customer; don't misrepresent anything. We're not that kind of business. People who lie to make money don't work here. Hopefully I've managed to build a reputation for our dealership that's one of integrity.

We've found that the best path is to be as straightforward as you can be. I work for a guy who I would not consider to be a believer, but he does absolutely the right thing and makes an honest profit. It's the same philosophy for all of our stores. We do things that are morally correct. I've been with this company since 1985. I'd hesitate to move somewhere else, because I know the philosophy behind this is that we're going to do things right.

I think my faith affects my job a lot. It helps me steer the organization in a way that I'm proud of. Probably half of my management staff are believers, as well as a number of my sales people and a number of my mechanics. We seem to hire that type of person.

I also have the opportunity to talk to people in ways I can't even begin to describe. Advertising salespeople, for instance—they come in to sell me something, and before they leave, they're telling me their life story and where they're hurting. We end up talking about where they go to church, what's going on in their life. There's a challenge to that, because I have to balance my time. My boss would not look favorably on my spending an hour talking to somebody about Christianity. So I've got to somehow walk that fence. But it's phenomenal the opportunities God has dropped in my lap.

If a kid was motivated and energetic when he got out of high school, he could walk into a car dealership and earn $35,000 to $100,000 in his first year. He's got to be willing to work evenings, weekends, a rotating schedule. If you want to work five days a week, it's the wrong business for you. There are also lots of jobs for mechanical technicians; those guys make $45,000 to $60,000 a year. If you're a good technician who can get the job done in less than the average amount of time, you can make a lot of money. Body-shop technicians can make good money too. If you're in accounting, you can work in an office in a car dealership and make about $50,000 and up, depending on how big the store is.

The car business is a pretty good field.

BARBARA KLOCKE
Senior Research Technician

I work in the research lab at a medical school and assist the director and his staff in their research. I manage a colony of about eight hundred mice, but I have to be cautious of how much I say about my mice work when I'm out in the public. There are some animal-rights activists out there, and there have been demonstrations at the university.

After I got my B.S. degree, I went on to what is now Truman State University in Missouri, where I got my master of science in biology. There I worked with flying squirrels out in the field. That helped me really comprehend scientific processes. I was in a position where I had to think for myself and implement everything on my own. It made all of the science come alive for me.

It was my love of animals that got me into biology. In high school I wanted to be a zoo director. Unfortunately doors did not open in that area. After my freshman year at college, I tried to get a job at a zoo in Springfield, Illinois, but they wouldn't hire someone who didn't live in the area.

By the time I finished college, I knew I wasn't going to be a zoo director, so getting my master's helped me clarify what I did want to do. That's also when I got a job in the medical school, working with transgenic mice. My job is working on cell pathways in the brain during development. Cells are constantly dying and growing, but when cells don't get the message to die, that's when tumors form. If you can understand all the pieces in the puzzle that help genes die, you can treat them with gene therapy or drugs.

In my actual work I can't see a direct role for my Christian faith. Indirectly everything I do is God-centered. And I do my best in my work because of my Christian beliefs. You get to work with a lot of people with different faiths. There's definitely a chance to share your faith with others.

My goal right now is to stay in one lab long enough to make a difference with the research. In science it takes a while to do the research. Being a technician, you don't get your own project to work on; you're part of a team working for the lab's director. If you're in place long enough, you can earn the respect of your boss.

My advice? Take notice of what interests you. Then use that interest to help guide you.

JIM HUGHES
Management Company Developer

I'm what we call a program manager—basically, a developer. For instance, the Green Bay Packers needed a bigger, better stadium, so my company was brought in to help them hire an architect, hire a contractor, and then run through the whole project with them. We're pretty much a management company; we don't really do anything except manage. We hire people to do the work, so we're constantly holding meetings to keep everybody coordinated and directed. I'm in meetings all day. I see the phenomenon where everybody thinks they want to do this job. Then companies come in and the people say, "Oh, we have to do *that?*" or "I don't want to deal with *that.*"

I kind of got into construction from the technical/science/engineering side, but the reality is that the job is mostly about people. You can solve the technical problems. But it's the people who keep it interesting for me. It's probably like any normal office situation involving people, except we go to a different project every year or two, so there's a whole different group of people that you have to deal with every couple of years.

I went to Purdue University in Indiana with the idea of being an aeronautical/aerospace engineer. But that industry wasn't hiring then. So for some weird reason, I gravitated toward construction. The funny thing is that by the time I graduated, aerospace engineers were in demand and construction was in the dumps. So maybe the moral is to do what you want and let the details work themselves out later.

My first job was in Elgin, Illinois, where I worked for an excavation contractor. Then I went on to build schools and jails in Indianapolis. We moved to Arizona, and I built some buildings for the University of Arizona, and then a federal courthouse. Next, we built Miller Park in Milwaukee—the stadium with the retractable roof—and now we're expanding the Packers' stadium, putting in new suites and adding office space.

If I get frustrated at work, all I have to do is go outside and look at the building. If you're a preacher, say you give a sermon, teach people, lead classes, but you really don't know if they're listening or if your words are going to have an effect on people's lives. I don't know how they keep going. I can go outside or go up on a building and say, "This is what we're doing. This is what it's all about." And I know this building will, theoretically, be there for the next hundred years. Or at least until the next construction crew comes along!

My faith is real important. It goes back to the people issue: It's so easy to compromise and just go with the flow when you're working with people. But one of my secrets is to look at it this way: My employer is not who I'm worried about; I have to do what's right because I have to answer to God. A lot of times I find myself going against the flow. In the end that's the secret of my success. Construction can be real cutthroat. But people who are honest and keep their word tend to rise to the top.

I tell college kids that even though your professors might not be very good, they're still looking out for your best interests. In business it's just the opposite. But the thing that Christ taught is that the leader is a servant. You've got to be truthful and honest, and you can't lord it over people. If you do those things, people will know you're trying to do the best thing.

I like doing these big jobs. The biggest drawback, though, is having to move so much, which is hard on Pam, my wife. Three or four years is the longest I've ever worked with a company. Some of that's because companies change: Businesses get bigger and smaller, lay people off, pick people up. But it's also because I keep hearing the siren song of the "bigger job." Partly because of that, there's no sense of security. I'm not looking to depend on some company or some pension plan for my job security. I look to Christ.

ERIN SIMS
Medical Claims Adjuster

I graduated from high school, went to college for two and a half years, and then started working full time at a company called Attenta as a medical-only claims adjuster for workers' compensation. I'm on the phone a lot, talking mostly with the employers of people who were injured and with attorneys.

I just did not enjoy school. I quit because I didn't know what I wanted to do in life. I thought, *Why not just quit school and go back when I know what I want to do?* I believe I could have gone right into this job without any college. But everybody tells me every single day that I made the biggest mistake of my life by quitting school. I *know* that in my head, but I just don't *feel* it right now. I'm just not a school person. I do hope to go back at some time.

I thought I wanted to go into nursing, so I went to work in a doctor's office. That allowed me to see what nursing might be like, and I decided it was not for me. I didn't like all of the paperwork. When I was in high school, I volunteered at a hospital in Birmingham, and we did more hands-on work with the patients, which I preferred. In the future I think I might like to be a social worker.

I may be here for a long time, I don't know. It's a wonderful company. But I'm more of a hands-on type person.

Most people I went to high school with have never had a job. I do feel more mature than some of them who went to college. I'm a grownup. I've already started investing money and saving for retirement. I feel like I know how to take the real world. I know what to expect because I'm "out there."

As far as my faith goes, I try to keep a positive attitude at work. When people are talking, I try to come back with something—not necessarily Christian, but positive. I think my coworkers knew from the first day that I was different. I feel like that's a witness right there.

My advice: If you're not sure what you want to do, try to go to work in the environment you're considering. That can help narrow your options down.

I've known people who've done horrible in high school and loved college.

And I know people who did well in high school and hated college. So if you're not sure about whether to go or not, I'd just say, "Go and try it out."

Bryan Hitch

Pastor of Worship and Media Ministries, Christian Recording Artist, Freelance Musician

My parents recognized when I was about three or four that I could hear a melody and play it on the piano. Before piano lessons, I could play "Heart and Soul" because I heard my dad play it. At five years old I started taking piano lessons, and I took them for eleven years. When I was six years old, we started singing together as a family as a hobby. Because I grew up in that environment and had natural and/or God-given abilities, it was what I did best. So that's what I pursued. I got involved in choirs and bands in junior high and high school. In my junior year of high school, I discovered that it was possible to do this for a living.

My family group, The Hitches, recorded an album in 1983. My brother and I had begun to write original music, and it was at that point we thought we might be writing songs that other people would want to hear. So we started putting tapes together and sending them to record companies. I pursued getting "discovered" and getting a record deal.

And I got rejected. Emotionally it is disappointing when you get that letter saying, "Good, but not what we're looking for." That whole process is such a who-you-know kind of thing. A couple years out of college, I was haunted by how things might have been different had I gone to school in Nashville. If I had relocated and started to network, my life might have followed a different course. But you can't live life based on "could have been"/"should have been." And things might not have been any different. I could have gone to Tennessee, met all the right people, and it might not have happened anyway.

When my brother and I were turned down for a record deal, we asked, "What should we do? Who should we pursue?" We heard Jack Hayford speak at a musicians' conference, and his thing was, "Don't make a record deal the savior of your ministry. Make Jesus the Savior of your ministry. If a record deal happens, you'll know it's because you were pursuing the right thing." We turned a corner as a family at that point.

After college I held various part-time self-employed jobs so I could pursue music. I had to work at construction and painting so I could travel and sing on the weekends with my family. I was able to pursue what I wanted to pursue, but I had to do other things—"waiting tables," I call it. For instance, I had contact with a guy in college who was instrumental in my ability to earn extra income as a songwriter, musician, arranger, and producer. I recorded and produced arrangements for theme parks and did arranging on CD projects for other artists. That helped me pursue a full-time music ministry even when it wasn't paying all of the bills.

Around 1983 we formed a fourteen-piece band, so our weekend travels at that time involved riding in two or three vans, with a truck for all of the equipment. Sometimes we'd do things like end a gig on Sunday night in Chicago, then drive all night to get back to Columbus so those who had to go to work on Monday would be able to sleep. Sometimes we were doing sixteen concerts a month. That falls under the heading of "Doing what you have to do."

From 1983 to 1991 we made fifteen recordings. They were pretty much sold at concerts. The limited bookstore sales we had were mostly in Columbus.

In 1991 I began to pursue solo dates because most of my family was heading in different directions, and I wanted to pursue music full time. In 1992 I recorded my first solo project. I did four CDs between '92 and '98. I toured a national schedule, out for five or six weeks at a time, and I always traveled to the West Coast at least once a year. Most of my concentrated dates were in the Midwest, but I went as far south as Florida. Once I was on my own and could fly, I could be in New Mexico one week, North Carolina the next. From 1991 to 2000 I went wherever the door was open.

In the latter stages of traveling and ministry, I got to the point where I was making enough money that I could be a little more choosy with the dates I played. This allowed me more time to be home and involved in my local church. I'd be gone most of the summer, but I'd be home enough on weekends to be the worship leader at my church. I was also chairman of the deacon board, holding a leadership position that really grounded me.

At that point my wife and I were homeschooling because I traveled all the time. But my son decided he wanted to go to high school; his cousins had really good experiences at high school. When we decided together that would be his option, I realized I was going to have a shift in vocation. If he was going to be in high school, I knew I was going to settle down into a more stay-put position. The natural progression was to become a worship leader at a church.

Initially I thought the transition to a staff job would be much more of a disappointment than it was. Some of that was age-driven: I felt like I'd held on to that youthful, free-spirit kind of deal, and now I was going to be confined. Then I discovered there were things about this job that were exciting and stimulating. Being with the same worship team every week, rehearsing with the band, seeing the same faces every Sunday—I didn't know these would be such blessings until I got involved.

I was concerned that my four kids wouldn't adjust well from the "road" life to the community life. We went from homeschooling them all to having them all involved in public school.

Every week I get to do what I like best and what I'm gifted at and make a living and support my family. That's still incredible to me. I get to rehearse every week with musicians and vocalists, to work at becoming better and better at what we do, to see people's lives changed both from discipling and from the reality of the gospel. The surprise has been the opportunity to work on a staff team, to interact and share in the pastoral responsibilities. It's the first time I've ever had a boss—and the good news is that he's wonderful. He allows me to do what I need to do to get the job done.

I've also been able to pursue some concerts and extracurricular activities—like writing all the music for an interactive children's CD. I think that's God's way of telling me I can still pursue some of what I loved about being a free-lance musician and singer.

Advice: Absolutely get all the information and education you can get about what you want to do. To pursue what I pursued did not require a college education. I could have easily done all that I've done without it. But at college, I gained social and interpersonal relationships, and it's where I met my wife. I also made some connections at college that ended up accounting for 40 to 50 percent of my income in some of the early years. Today you can actually find a school where you can pursue a career as a contemporary Christian musician and study studio arranging and stuff like that. That wasn't available when I was a student.

Enjoy every part of the journey. Getting hung up on trying to reach something you never attain can be a very discouraging process. But if you're in this small group that only sings at local churches, enjoy doing it for whatever period of time it lasts.

MICHELLE NAUMANN
Instructor of English as a Second Language (ESL)

After I graduated from college, I taught for two semesters and then got my master's degree in teaching English as a Second Language (ESL). I have been teaching ESL ever since.

Most of my ESL classes are filled with adult students. I usually have between eight and twenty students in a class, and they probably speak five to fifteen different primary languages. They all have different reasons for being there. Maybe their English isn't good enough for them to take a regular English class. Maybe they're having a hard time being understood at work, or they need better English to find work.

I *really* enjoy the students. I love learning about their different cultures, food, languages, and viewpoints. International people are very intelligent and respectful and willing and eager to learn. And they still have a vision for American freedom and liberty, something that we sometimes just take for granted.

Believe it or not, I also really love grammar! In fact, I'm writing a textbook on grammar.

I first started teaching shortly after I became a Christian, and I was a lot more on fire then than I am now. I try to show my faith, though, by being moral and ethical in my teaching—doing my best and being prepared. I'm also open about my faith when students ask. Once, some Saudi students were talking about observing Ramadan, and they asked if I ever fasted in my religion. I told them that in Christianity some people fast to draw closer to God, but that it wasn't a requirement or anything. I also give out my home phone number to students and tell them that they can call me any day but Sunday, when I'm at church. So that's opened up discussions about what kind of church I go to and what I believe.

People have told me that I have the gift of teaching. If I weren't teaching, I'd probably be some kind of missionary, working in some way with international people.

KEITH JOHNSON
Moderator/Chaplain

After college I went to Northern Baptist Theological Seminary, then I got a B.A. in broadcasting, then a master's in counseling, a master's in divinity, and then my doctorate. After school I worked with the homeless for about twelve years. You really see God when you work with people in the streets.

During those twelve years I also wrote a couple of books, and I was traveling all the time to speak and to promote them. The street ministry and everything else really took a toll on me and on my ministry with my family. My wife finally divorced me as a result.

After I took that turn in my ministry, I resettled. For about two years I traveled to promote my current book, and I tried to reassess my life. I realized that I was pushing hard to be successful, but that success is really a matter of where your heart is.

Then I was hired by a company to counsel missionaries who were depressed. I was like a consultant working with missionaries. They sent me all over the world. I traveled to Rome, Paris, Switzerland, the Dominican Republic. My job was to help missionaries understand themselves and adjust to their new cultures. Once I finished running around the world, I decided to return home, where I established a private counseling practice for a year. Then I was asked to work at the school where I am now. I learned not to be married to the ministry but to be married to the Lord.

Currently I'm a moderator/chaplain at a private Christian school. I encourage students to develop their relationship with God.

We have three hundred students. We're most prone to get kids who haven't made it in the public schools. And not just kids. We have parents, even teachers, with problems. Drugs, alcohol, trouble with the law. There isn't a day that goes by when I don't have to solve a crisis.

Every Friday I lead a Bible study at school. I can put all my talents to work and be there to help. The Christian message is the string that holds everything together here. For instance, if I'm teaching a kid world history at home—because he isn't able to handle being in class—I'm constantly sharing Christ's love with him and his family. No matter how many different things I do, everything comes back to a point of ministry.

My advice would be to get to know your talents. Take time to look for your purpose. It's for your sake and God's. I pursued my talents, and they took me to the streets, helped me travel the world, and put me in a great school now. I know I'm where I'm supposed to be. But I was *guided* more than I *chose*.

Notes

Chapter 1

1. From the November 2001 *Monthly Labor Review,* published by the Bureau of Labor Statistics.

Chapter 2

1. Dorothy L. Sayers, "Why Work?" in *Creed or Chaos?* (Manchester, N.H.: Sophia Institute Press, 1974), 76.
2. Sayers, "Why Work?" 73.

Chapter 3

1. Ken Lawson, *K.I.S.S. Guide to Managing Your Career* (New York: Dorling Kindersley Publishing, 2000), 109-10.

Chapter 5

1. Peter McWilliams, *Do It! Let's Get Off Our Buts* (Los Angeles: Prelude Press, 1994), 23.

Chaper 7

1. Laurie Beth Jones, *The Path* (New York: Hyperion, 1996), 19.
2. Ted Conover, *Rolling Nowhere* (New York: Penguin Books, 1984), 24.

Chapter 8

1. Lawson, *K.I.S.S.,* 364.

Resources
(And Other Stuff You'll Only Read
If You're Desperate)

Step into a bookstore or wander online around www.bn.com or www.amazon. com, and it won't take you long to discover that shelves (real and virtual) are overflowing with books about getting a job and managing your career. There's no way I could possibly list and evaluate them all here, even if I wanted to.

And that's just the books. Add Web sites, hotlines, and small-group meetings across the country, and it's enough to make your lips tingle. (And not in a good way.)

So the following resources represent just a small sampling of what's available to you. Hopefully they can get you started, point you in the right direction, or highlight something you weren't aware of before. Some have been useful in the writing of this book; others are just good, reliable places to turn for information, leads, and so on.

One final note: Some of these books are out of print—or soon will be. But if a title looks like something you absolutely must get, don't be put off by the mere fact that it's out of print or can't be found on the shelves of your local mall bookstore. Many thousands (millions?) of out-of-print books can be found in used bookstores and online through such sites as www.abebooks.com and www.alibris.com. (Yes, you can also order out-of-print and used books through Amazon.com, but you'll pay more for them.)

Unfortunately, the same situation does not apply to defunct Web sites or links that have broken because their hosts have moved on to bigger and better things (like starting high school or something). However, the sheer scope of the Web pretty much guarantees that other, similar sites will still be around to answer your questions and meet your needs. To find them, I'd recommend using Google (www.google.com) to search for pages with keywords and phrases.

Books

Career Clues for the Clueless by Christopher D. Hudson, Denise Kohlmeyer, and Randy Southern (Uhrichsville, Ohio: Promise Press, an imprint of Barbour Publishing, 1999). A small-format guide packed with basic tips for on-the-job success, from descriptions of more than thirty careers to how to deal with sexual harassment and job loss—all presented in bite-size paragraphs and shaded boxes.

The Complete Idiot's Guide to Making Money in Freelancing by Laurie E. Rozakis, Ph.D. (New York: Alpha Books, 1998). "Freelancing" may sound like "freelance *writing*," but Rozakis's focus is much broader than that. This book is for everyone who wants to be their own boss. If you're not quite sure what's involved in running your own business, this book is a great place to start. It explains the fundamentals—from learning why you might want to freelance, creating a business plan, and setting up your office—but it also goes into detail about running your business successfully, including negotiation strategies, bookkeeping, taxes, and expansion. Laurie Rozakis has also coauthored *The Complete Idiot's Guide to Office Politics* with Bob Rozakis.

Cool Careers for Dummies by Marty Nemko, Paul Edwards, and Sarah Edwards (Foster City, Calif.: John Wiley & Sons, IDG Books, 2001). (Yeah, we go from "idiots" to "dummies.") Offers helpful advice on how to get a job, presented in the proven "Dummies" format. Still, there are better general career books out there. More than one hundred pages are devoted to the "Cool Careers Yellow Pages" (and they are, in fact, yellow), but it seems like wasted space if you already have some inkling of what you want to do. And if you don't, the assessment tools here probably won't help all that much.

Creating a Life Worth Living by Carol Lloyd (New York: HarperCollins, 1997). Based on Lloyd's popular seminar series, this book is especially targeted to readers who are interested in more "creative" occupations— in her words, "aspiring artists, innovators, and entrepreneurs." Filled with interviews with creative types—including a painter, a short-story writer, a musician, a performance artist, a designer, an inventor—the book takes readers from developing a creative vision to pursuing a wholly creative life. As a nonfiction writer, I didn't find it particularly helpful. But if you're leaning toward a creative or arts-based occupation, it's worth checking out.

Discover What You're Best At by Linda Gale (New York: Simon & Schuster, Fireside, 1990). The subtitle is *A Complete Career System That Lets You Test Yourself to Discover Your Own True Career Abilities,* and the book lives up to that lofty claim. If you have any questions at all about where your real gifts and interests lie, get this book. If you're feeling a little dissatisfied in your current job or in your current course of study at school, get this book. If you're—aw, just get this book. You won't regret it.

Do It! Let's Get Off Our Buts by Peter McWilliams (Los Angeles: Prelude Press, 1994). A very easy-to-read but incredibly inspirational book for setting aside negative attitudes and following your dreams in every aspect of your life (not just in your career).

The *First Year* Career Series (New York: Walker and Company, various years). Each of the five books currently in this series offers nearly two dozen first-person stories of "first jobs" in specific careers. For those curious about the hurdles and the high points that accompany a specific career choice, these stories will be entertaining and insightful. Books include *My First Year as a Doctor, My First Year as a Journalist, My First Year as a Lawyer, My First Year in Book Publishing,* and *The First Year of Teaching.*

Gig: Americans Talk About Their Jobs, edited by John Bowe, Marisa Bowe, and Sabin Streeter (New York: Three Rivers Press, 2001). A compilation of uncensored first-person stories that originally appeared as "Work" columns in the Webzine *Word.* If you were ever curious about what a particular job might *really* look like, these essays can be invaluable. A few famous contributors crop up, but most are just regular folks doing jobs that include Wal-Mart greeter, crime-scene cleaner, and tofu manufacturer. Be forewarned: A lot of the folks here don't seem to actually like what they're doing.

The Insider's Guide to the Colleges, compiled and edited by the staff of the *Yale Daily News* (New York: St. Martin's Press, annual). While any number of guides can point you to a good school, the *Insider's* approach is to include information and opinions from students who are actually there. The result really *does* feel like an insider's take on each school. Although many, many worthwhile schools are not represented here (including my own alma mater), the selection includes lots of helpful data on small regional colleges as well as major universities. Browse the index before picking this one up; if even half of the schools you're considering are listed there, you'll find this book well worth the seventeen dollars (or whatever).

K.I.S.S. Guide to Managing Your Career by Ken Lawson (New York: Dorling Kindersley Publishing, 2000). Pick this one up. While its four-color design and highly graphic layout may look light and breezy, this is the most well-rounded and useful general-interest one-volume book on careers that I have ever seen. Includes personal-interest surveys, résumé and interview how-tos, and career-management tips you will still be using years from now.

Make Millions Doing Absolutely Nothing! Wow, you're actually reading all of this stuff. You know, when writers are sitting at home trying to come up with lots of really practical, helpful information, we have to wonder if anyone out there is paying attention. Our fear is that you're reading along, the phone rings, and you flip to these back pages so you can quickly write down somebody's number or a message about what to pick up at the grocery story without getting off the couch and hunting down a piece of paper. So thank you for easing my mind! I appreciate it! (And if, by some *freak* of chance, you just happened to read this while you were scribbling something like "frozen yogurt, spaghetti sauce, bird food, that weird snack thing Dad likes" in the margin, I'd rather not know. Really.)

Nice Job: The Guide to Cool, Odd, Risky, and Gruesome Ways to Make a Living by The Lookout Media Team (Berkeley, Calif.: Ten Speed Press, 1999). The title pretty much says it all. This book includes interviews and job specifics for an eclectic range of occupations, from pet groomer to Publishers Clearinghouse "Prize Patrol" member, with stripper and executioner tossed in along the way. If your career thinking tends to stop at "police officer, lawyer, doctor," this book will open your eyes to the wide range of possibilities out there.

Nickel and Dimed: On (Not) Getting By in America by Barbara Ehrenreich (New York: Henry Holt, Owl Books, 2001). Based on the author's attempt to see whether "real" people can actually live on entry-level wages, this book follows her experiment from Florida to Maine to Minnesota. The results are not entirely convincing. She gave herself a month in each place to find employment and a place to live, yet she always knew she had a "real" life to return to—and backup money in the bank. In addition, some readers may not appreciate the author's language, her politics, or her attitudes toward religion. However, the hard truth is that Ehrenreich could *not* survive on one job alone—and that two jobs were often still not enough to keep even a bad roof over her head. This is an eye-opening report from the front lines of the working poor.

The Path: Creating Your Mission Statement for Work and for Life by Laurie Beth Jones (New York: Hyperion, 1996). A small book offering a thoroughly Christian approach to creating a mission statement that will guide career choices as well as life decisions. Includes exercises, meditations, and numerous case histories drawn from the Bible and from the author's seminars.

The 7 Habits of Highly Effective People by Stephen R. Covey (New York:
  Simon & Schuster, Fireside, 1989). This may be a contemporary classic,
  but it's worth reading anyway! Covey draws on his strong moral
  approach to life—he's writing from a Mormon perspective—and real-
  world business experience to help readers prioritize their career concerns
  and choices and establish career paths that support their fundamental
  spiritual needs. The principles he offers are timeless and, um, effective.

Whistle While You Work: Heeding Your Life's Calling by Richard J. Leider and
  David A. Shapiro (San Francisco: Berrett-Koehler Publishers, 2001).
  While not specifically Christian, this book offers exercises and interviews
  related to finding your calling and living out a spiritually meaningful
  career.

Work-at-Home Options by Joanne Cleaver (Elgin, Ill.: Chariot, LifeJourney
  Books, 1994). Primarily targeted to stay-at-home Christian moms, this
  book does offer practical advice and encouragement for everyone who is
  self-employed.

Working in the Dark: Keeping Your Job While Dealing with Depression by
  Fawn Fitter and Beth Gulas (Center City, Minn.: Hazelden, 2002). Not
  a "career book" per se, but a useful handbook for any of the estimated
  eleven million Americans who experience a major episode of depression
  every year—many of them younger adults. The focus is on handling job
  responsibilities (or explaining to colleagues and managers why you can't)
  while facing your depression and getting the help you need to come
  through it successfully.

You Can Be Anything! From A to Z by Sarah Montague (New York: Villard
  Books, 2002). If you are easily offended or don't have a cynical bone in
  your body, stay away. Everyone else: Try out the first alphabetical entry,
  "Amy is adopted." If you don't think it's funny, it's not for you, either.
  But if you laugh, read on. (You can finish the book in about ten minutes standing in the bookstore. Call your friends over and read it aloud
  to them. But not too loud or you'll get kicked out.) There is no redeem-

ing quality to this book, just a twisted and often hilarious look at what we can or might become in life if we're not careful. Consider it a quick break from the reality of career concerns.

Your Career in Changing Times by Lee Ellis and Larry Burkett (Chicago: Moody, 1993). Helps readers tie their career "into the larger picture of pursuing God's will through efficient use of one's gifts." Includes psychological assessment tools and advice for conducting a job search, preparing cover letters and résumés, establishing a budget, and planning for retirement. However, it is written primarily for people who have been in the job market for some time and are now changing course.

Your Job: Survival or Satisfaction? by Jerry and Mary White (Grand Rapids: Zondervan, 1977). Okay, this book is *way* old. But if you're interested in learning more about being an effective Christian in a secular workplace, you'll find some useful stuff here. It can sound old-fashioned in places (it was probably out of date in 1977), and it takes an "us-versus-them" attitude toward Christians and their non-Christian coworkers (which I don't agree with), but I think it's worth checking out nonetheless. If you can find it somewhere for a buck or two, consider picking it up.

WEB RESOURCES

Job Sites

You may be tempted to start your search with one of the major job clearinghouses on the Web, such as www.monster.com. That's probably not your best bet. If you know that you're looking for a job in a particular industry, track down the trade association that serves that industry. Then visit their Web site. They will likely offer job links that will be far more targeted to your specialty than anything you'll see right away on the general-interest sites. (Some association sites may require registration or even a paid membership before you can access job listings. Many offer less-expensive memberships to students, however.)

For example, if you were interested in a job at a newspaper, you could check out the listings sponsored by *American Journalism Review* (www.ajr.org), the Society of Professional Journalists (www.spj.org), the National Writers Union (www.nwu.org), and JournalismJobs.com.

If, on the other hand, you were interested in jobs in earth science, the Web site Geology One (www.geologyone.com/assoclinks.htm#associations) lists over a dozen relevant associations in the United States alone—from the American Association of Petroleum Geologists (www.aapg.org) to the Society of Vertebrate Paleontology (www.vertpaleo.org). The day I visited, the Geological Society of America (www.geosociety.org) listed fifteen open positions at their site, from a geomorphologist to volcanology assistantships.

You get the idea.

If you don't know where to start, go to www.google.com and type in "associations" and your general field of interest (for instance, "science" or "construction" or "medical"). Chances are you'll get more hits than you'll know what to do with. Once you've explored these special-interest job opportunities, then I'd say it's time to visit the following, more general-interest sites and see what they have to offer.

- *altavista.worklife.com*—A richly stocked starting place for your job search, including career information for the self-employed. (Note that this site's URL doesn't include the usual "www" prefix.)

- *chronicle.com/jobs*—Because this is the *Chronicle of Higher Education*'s career network, the emphasis is on jobs in colleges and universities, although other kinds of positions are represented. There is also information related to careers in general, changing course midcareer, and landing your first job. (Note that this site's URL doesn't include the usual "www" prefix.)

- *www.americasemployers.com*—The home of Net Temps, a general-interest job site specializing in, but not limited to, temporary and contract jobs.

- *www.asktheheadhunter.com*—The "insider's edge on job search and hiring."

- *www.careerbuilder.com*—Despite the URL, this is more of a job-finding site than a guide to career management. "Over 400,000 Better Jobs!" it claims. (I'll leave the conclusions up to you.)

- *www.christianet.com/christianjobs*—A fairly good site for finding ministry-related positions. Some employers ask that you raise all or most of your "support" (read: "salary").

- *www.christianjobs.com*—A very professional-looking resource offering job listings and career information for employers, ministries, and job hunters alike. Registration and "membership" are required to take advantage of all of the site's features.

- *www.juniorjobs.com*—This site focuses on part-time and summer-job listings for high-school students in the mid-Atlantic states (Maryland, North Carolina, Virginia, West Virginia, and Washington, D.C.).

- *www.monster.com*—A huge job-listing site covering all job categories across the United States.

- *www.usajobs.opm.gov*—Job opportunities with the Federal Government, along with résumé-building tools, an online application, and employment facts and tips.

Managing Your Career

- *www.asktheemployer.com*—Offers career-management advice in a wide range of areas. Also offers an "e-Mentor" service that links users with more experienced colleagues.

- *www.assessment.com*—The Web home of the Motivational Appraisal of Personal Potential (MAPP) assessment tools.

- *www.bls.gov/oco/cg/home.htm*—The Career Guide to Industries, an encyclopedic description of careers available in every major industry imaginable. Published by the U.S. Department of Labor's Bureau of Labor Statistics.

- *www.careerjournal.com*—A *Wall Street Journal*–supported site full of articles, advice, and other career-building information.

- *www.careershop.com/careerdr*—Go to Careershop.com and you'll find a basic site for job searches and résumé building. But add the "careerdr" extension and you'll be able to tap the expertise of the Career Dr., Dr. Randall Hansen. Read past Q&As with the doctor or ask for advice yourself.

- *www.dol.gov*—Home page of the U.S. Department of Labor, offering links to a seemingly bottomless well of practical information, statistics, and employment projections.

- *www.iccweb.com*—The Internet Career Connection. Includes links to dozens of career-building resources, including networking and self-employment.

- *www.rileyguide.com*—A combination job and career site that offers many useful resources.

- *www.shrm.org*—Home page of the Society for Human Resource Management. Offers a wealth of job-related news, information, and resources, including selected articles from *HR Magazine,* the trade magazine for HR professionals.

Acknowledgments

This book would never have seen the light of day had it not been for all of the people at Shaw Books who encouraged and supported it at every stage of the process, from proposal to printed, bound book. I especially want to thank Don Pape for playing the role of enthusiastic publisher, Elisa Stanford for her editorial oversight and encouragement along the way, and Jennifer Lonas for her careful handling of the copyediting. You all have my sincere thanks and my undying gratitude.

Dozens of friends, acquaintances, and total strangers took time away from their work and leisure moments to talk openly with me about their jobs. Some ended up being quoted by name in the book itself, but some didn't. At the risk of leaving someone out, I want to specifically thank Tara Greenway, Bryan Hitch, Jim Hughes, Keith Johnson, Barbara Klocke, Michelle Naumann, Nathan Potratz, Glynda Rice, Erin Sims, John Welch, Eric Woolbright, Rebecca Miles Risser, Mike Moore, Rosie Oatman, Traci Steffen, Erica Vonderheid, Christina Xenos, JoyAnne Oatman, Jeanneane Palczewski, Pam Hughes, and Steve and Debbie Layne. Whether you realized it or not, you all helped to make this a better book.

I also want to recognize four people who have played a more behind-the-scenes role in helping me think about and produce this book:

Dr. Charles W. Moore, my former pastor and now the president of Northern Baptist Theological Seminary in Lombard, Illinois;

Elizabeth Johnson, a friend and fellow freelance writer who never seems to mind helping me improve what I've written;

My wife, Sylvia, for her understanding and companionship;

And finally, my mother, Lois Bittner. In many very real ways, this book could not have been written without her love and support.

About the Author

ROBERT BITTNER worked in marketing and editorial for sixteen years before becoming a full-time freelance editor and writer focusing on book and magazine writing. He is the author of several books, including *Under His Wings: Meeting the Spiritual Needs of the Mentally Disabled,* and he is currently a board member of the American Society of Journalists and Authors (ASJA). Bittner's magazine nonfiction has appeared in a diverse range of publications including *Preservation, Pages, The Writer, Family Circle, Moody, The Christian Reader, Catholic Digest,* and *Christianity Today.* He and his wife, Sylvia, live in Michigan with their two cats, Scout and Boo.

Bob would love to hear from readers who have found their perfect jobs or who would just like to share their own career stories (and maybe wind up in a future book). Write to him at YPJ@robertbittner.com.

Printed in the United States
by Baker & Taylor Publisher Services